$29.95

D1520970

TODAY'S WRITERS
AND THEIR WORKS

BILL
BRYSON

Scott P. Richert

Marshall Cavendish
Benchmark
New York

Other Marshall Cavendish Offices:
Marshall Cavendish International (Asia) Private Limited, 1 New Industrial Road, Singapore
536196 • Marshall Cavendish International (Thailand) Co Ltd. 253 Asoke, 12th Flr,
Sukhumvit 21 Road, Klongtoey Nua, Wattana, Bangkok 10110, Thailand
Marshall Cavendish (Malaysia) Sdn Bhd, Times Subang, Lot 46, Subang Hi-Tech
Industrial Park, Batu Tiga, 40000 Shah Alam, Selangor Darul Ehsan, Malaysia
Marshall Cavendish is a trademark of Times Publishing Limited
All websites were available and accurate when this book was sent to press.

Library of Congress Cataloging-in-Publication Data
Richert, Scott P. • Bill Bryson / by Scott P. Richert.
p. cm. — (Today's writers and their works) • Includes bibliographical references.
Summary: "A biography of writer Bill Bryson that describes his era,
major works, and life"—Provided by publisher.
ISBN 978-0-7614-4120-5
1. Bryson, Bill—Juvenile literature. 2. Travel writers—United States—Biography—Juvenile
literature. 3. Travel writers—England—Biography—Juvenile literature. I. Title.
G154.5.B79R53 2010 • 910.4092—dc22 • [B] • 2008055989

Publisher: Michelle Bisson • Art Director: Anahid Hamparian
Series Designer: Alicia Mikles • Photo research by Lindsay Aveilhe

The photographs in this book are used by permission and through the courtesy of:
Rick Friedman/Corbis: cover; Dave Caulkin/AP Photo: 4; Iowa State
University Press: 8; Popperfoto/Getty Images: 8; Christopher Furlong/Getty Images: 19;
Helicopter Tjungurrayi. Pikarti Soak, 1998. Acrylic on Canvas. Courtesy of the artist and
Warlayirti Artists. © 2009 Artists Rights Society (ARS), New York / VISCOPY, Australia: 25;
Newscom: 33; Keystone/Getty Images: 36; Bettmann/Corbis: 39, 42;
Retrofile/Getty Images: 42; Chris Hondros/Getty Images: 50; Bruce Dale/Getty Images: 60;
Rick Friedman/Corbis: 80; Hulton Archive/Getty Images: 88; Summer Pierre. Courtesy of
the artist. www.summerpierre.com: 92; Reproduced courtesy of Bonestell LLC: 95.

Printed in Malaysia (T)
135642

CONTENTS

Bill Bryson was born in Iowa, the American heartland, but he spent much of his adult life in Great Britain. In December 2003 he posed at Stonehenge after being appointed an English Heritage Commissioner.

LIFE

"I COME FROM DES MOINES. Somebody had to." With those words, Bill Bryson begins the first chapter of *The Lost Continent: Travels in Small-Town America* (1989), his first book to garner both popular and critical acclaim. It is as good a place as any to start an examination of the life of this well-known travel writer, columnist, memoirist, chronicler of language, biographer of Shakespeare, and historian of nearly everything. A modern-day expatriate who has spent most of his adult life in England, Bryson has worked as an editor for two of the most influential British newspapers and written the majority of his books while living overseas. To this day, however, he is almost always described in the British press as an American writer, and his youth in the American midwest of the 1950s and 1960s has clearly left its mark on his work.

Family Background and Childhood

William McGuire Bryson was born on December 8, 1951, in Mercy Hospital in Des Moines, Iowa. His parents, he writes in *The Life and Times of the Thunderbolt Kid: A Memoir,* "named him William, after his father. They would call him Billy until he was old enough to ask them not to." Thereafter, like his father, a renowned sportswriter for the *Des Moines Register*, Bryson would be known as Bill.

The third of three children, Bryson was considerably younger than his siblings. His sister, Mary Elizabeth (known as Betty), was five years older than Bill; his brother, Michael G. Bryson, with whom he shared a room until the latter went off to college, was nine years older. "They were big enough," Bryson writes in *Thunderbolt Kid*, "to be seldom around for most of my childhood." Indeed, his siblings are absent from most of Bryson's published reminiscences of his life through graduation from high school; in such books as *The Lost Continent* and *Thunderbolt Kid* they make the rare appearance, mainly in humorous anecdotes.

The Brysons were relatively well off, even by midwestern middle-class standards, which were quite comfortable at the time. As he writes in *Thunderbolt Kid*, "We . . . had a bigger house on a larger lot than most of my parents' colleagues. It was a white clapboard house with black shutters and a big screened porch atop a shady hill on the best side of town." Bryson credits the family's financial well-being to his mother's employment as the home-furnishings editor for the *Des Moines Register*. Up until the 1950s, the percentage of mothers in the United States who were employed outside of the home was relatively small, and most such arrangements were temporary, in order for the family to make ends meet. Mary McGuire Bryson's employment, Bryson writes in *Thunderbolt Kid*, presaged a change in the

American workforce, "in which husband and wife both went out to work to pay for a more ambitious lifestyle."

His mother's employment also signaled a certain freedom for young Billy, especially once his siblings had gone off on their own. In *Thunderbolt Kid* the author describes how he developed an independent streak and a certain aloofness as a child that later would be reflected strongly in his writing. Even his attendance at school, he claims (probably with some exaggeration), was somewhat sporadic, starting in kindergarten. "I was seldom asleep much before midnight, so when my mother called me in the morning, I usually found it inconvenient to rise," he writes in *Thunderbolt Kid*. "So I didn't go to school if I could help it."

Bryson often deprecates his own academic achievements; in fact, he sometimes gives the impression that it was a wonder that he graduated from elementary school. "As a scholar, I made little impact," he writes in *Thunderbolt Kid*. "My very first report card, for the first semester of first grade, had just one comment from the teacher: 'Billy talks in a low tone.'"

Becoming a Writer

Bryson read avidly as a child, starting with the Dick and Jane books, the primers that were a staple of post–World War II American education. He moved on to his family's *National Geographic* subscription and his father's home library, which featured "James Thurber, Robert Benchley, P. G. Wodehouse—all lightweight, middlebrow type stuff, but just perfect for me." Moreover, Bryson came by his writing skills naturally. His father was often on the road,

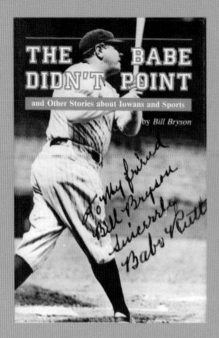

The expression "the apple doesn't fall very far from the tree" could easily apply to the Bryson brothers. Soon after the death of Bill Bryson Sr., Bill's older brother Michael, also a sportswriter, and his son edited a volume of their father's sports writing.

In post–World War II America, the creation of a nationwide interstate highway system gave rise to the explosion of family driving vacations in the 1950s.

especially on weekends, covering sports events—including, Bryson writes in *Thunderbolt Kid*, every World Series "from 1945 until his retirement" nearly forty years later. Indeed, at times, Bryson portrays his father more in his absence than in his presence. Still, it is clear that the elder Bryson's journalistic skills had a lasting influence on both of his sons. "During high school and college," Bryson told the *Independent* in 2001, "I worked on the local paper [the *Des Moines Register*] on evenings and at weekends." Bill's older brother, Michael, followed in his father's footsteps as a sportswriter. In 1989, three years after Bill Senior's death and about the same time that *The Lost Continent* appeared, Michael Bryson and his son edited a volume of Bill Bryson Sr.'s best sportswriting, *The Babe Didn't Point: And Other Stories about Iowans and Sports.*

The Lost Continent, which Bryson dedicated to his father, was occasioned by his father's death and recounts Bryson's attempt to retrace some of the family travels of his youth. While his father was an Iowa native, Bryson writes, "every year he became seized with a quietly maniacal urge to get out of the state and go on vacation." The 1950s and 1960s witnessed the explosive growth of a "car culture" in the United States; it was a time when summer vacations in station wagons without air conditioning became a staple of middle-class midwestern family life.

As Bryson describes them, his family's vacations consisted of long days in the car punctuated by short side trips to attractions that never quite measured up to the promise of roadside billboards. What Bryson never discusses in much detail and mentions only briefly in several books are the trips that he took with his father when the elder Bryson covered sports events (primarily baseball). "Because Dad was a sportswriter of some standing—no, to hell with the modesty, my dad was one of the finest sportswriters in the country and widely recognized as such—he could go into the press box and onto the field before the game and to his eternal credit he always took us with him."

In the introduction to *I'm a Stranger Here Myself: Notes on Returning to America after Twenty Years Away*, a collection of weekly columns that Bryson wrote for the Sunday magazine of the British *Mail on Sunday* newspaper after he and his family returned to the United States in 1995 to live in New Hampshire for several years, Bryson discusses the hassles of a weekly deadline. "The thing about a weekly column, I discovered, is that it comes up weekly. Now this may seem a self-evident fact, but in two years there never came a week when it did not strike me as both profound and startling." As a sportswriter for a daily newspaper, his father often dealt with deadlines that were measured in minutes, not days. When covering sporting events out of town in the days before fax machines and computers, the senior Bryson had to telephone the offices of the *Register* and dictate his stories to a typist on the other end of the line. Bryson often writes of his father's abilities with admiration: "At a time when most sportswriting was leaden or read as if written by enthusiastic but minimally gifted fourteen-year-olds," he writes in *Thunderbolt Kid*, "he wrote prose that was thoughtful, stylish, and comparatively sophisticated."

Discovering the Wider World

The elder Bryson's reputation brought him job offers from around the country, and as a child young Bill was always hopeful that the family would move. The opening lines of *The Lost Continent* are echoed in an interview that he gave to Norman Oder in *Publishers Weekly* in 1998: "Much as I resented having to grow up in Des Moines, it gave me a real appreciation for every place in the world that's not Des Moines."

In *Thunderbolt Kid*, Bryson describes growing up in Des Moines in the 1950s in much more glowing terms, but in his youth he held a different opinion. The first chapter of *The Lost Continent* describes his growing fascination with Europe as a child. A scene in a documentary from the early 1960s "showed Anthony Perkins walking along some sloping city street at dusk. I don't remember now if it was Rome or Paris, but the street was cobbled and shiny with rain and Perkins was hunched deep in a trench coat and I thought: 'Hey, *c'est moi!*'" Bryson was only about ten years old, but in his fascination with Europe, he was not alone, either in the 1950s and 1960s or in the broader scope of American history. Europe has always had a certain pull on Americans, especially on writers and others who are historically minded, and while modern America, with its technological marvels and "can do" attitude, had its charms for Bryson, those charms were not enough to keep him in Des Moines—or, for that matter, in the United States. "As soon as I was old enough I left. I left Des Moines and Iowa and the United States and the war in Vietnam and Watergate, and settled across the world."

Before leaving Des Moines, though, he graduated from Roosevelt High School and enrolled at Drake University. Drake was his mother's alma mater; indeed, she had been named Drake's homecoming queen in 1936. From 1969 to 1972, Bryson pursued his undergraduate degree at Drake, majoring in political science.

In the summer of 1972, Bryson made a journey that changed the course of his life. In pursuit of his dreams of seeing the Old Continent, he backpacked around Europe. "I still remember that first sight," he writes in the first chapter of his 1992 book *Neither Here nor There: Travels in Europe*. "The plane dropped out of the clouds, and there below me was this sudden magical tableau of small green fields and steepled villages spread across an undulating landscape, like a shaken-out quilt just settling back onto a bed." The contrast with America—particularly the American midwest —could not have been greater. "It was all so green and minutely cultivated, so compact, so tidy, so fetching, so . . . so European. I was smitten," he concludes. "I still am."

"It was," Bryson writes, "as happy a summer as I have ever spent." In the fall he returned to America but decided to take a semester off from his studies at Drake. The Continent continued to call him. He returned to Europe the next spring and made his way across the English Channel. "It was a foggy March night in 1973," he writes in *Notes from a Small Island: An Affectionate Portrait of Britain*, "when I arrived in Dover on the midnight ferry from Calais, having walked and hitchhiked from Luxembourg, where I had disembarked three days earlier from an Icelandic Airlines jet from New York." To say that it was love at first sight does not seem to be an exaggeration. Though Bryson's family roots were in Britain, as a child he had fallen in love with continental Europe. In his adulthood the British Isles supplanted continental Europe in his heart.

In April 1973 Bryson was joined in Europe by a friend from high school who is known throughout his writings by the pseudonym Stephen Katz. Katz is a prominent figure in both *Neither Here nor There* and *A Walk in the Woods: Rediscovering America on the Appalachian Trail*. In *Thunderbolt Kid*, Bryson describes first meeting Katz, "a transfer student from the Catholic school system," in the Audio-Visual Club at Callanan Junior High School in Des Moines. Though Bryson gave his friend a Jewish last name, he was actually Catholic. Bryson explained, "I chose the name Stephen Katz partly in honor of a Des Moines drugstore called Katz's, which was something of a local institution in my childhood, and partly because I wanted a short name that was easy to type."

Bryson and Katz spent much of the summer of 1973 quarreling (they quarreled often through the years) before finally parting ways in Istanbul, Turkey, in August. From there Bryson headed to London with the intention of returning home to resume his studies at Drake in the fall semester.

A Change of Course

Fate intervened. The night before he was scheduled to fly out of Heathrow Airport, in London, Bryson stayed in Virginia Water, Surrey, about twenty-six miles west-southwest of London. He was the guest of two student nurses from Des Moines who were working at the famous Holloway Sanatorium, a psychiatric institution outside of Virginia Water.

Named after Thomas Holloway, the nineteenth-century philanthropist who conceived of the sanatorium and financed its construction, Holloway Sanatorium is a massive structure that took twelve years to build and stands in the midst of twenty-four acres of parkland. Opened in 1885, it (along with Holloway College, designed by the same architect, W. H. Crossland) has been described by the architectural historians Ian Nairn and Sir Nikolaus Pevsner as the "summit of High Victorian design." After a fire in February 1978 damaged portions of the building, the sanatorium was closed in 1981.

The fire was in the future, however. In 1973 Holloway was looking for "menial staff," and the student nurses suggested that Bryson, "as a native speaker of English, was a shoo-in." Instead of catching his plane the next day, Bryson writes in *Notes from a Small Island*, "I found myself filling in forms and being told to present myself to the charge nurse on Tuke Ward at 7 a.m. the following morning."

Given the direction in which Bryson's career has taken him, it may seem surprising that his first employment in England was not in any way connected with writing. Of course, when he settled in England, he was only twenty-one years old and did not have a college degree. Suspending his studies at Drake indefinitely, Bryson first took seriously the idea of leaving the United States permanently. For twenty of the next twenty-two years, Bryson lived in England.

"It is an interesting experience to become acquainted with a country through the eyes of the insane, and, if I may say so, a particularly useful grounding for life in Britain," Bryson wrote in *Notes from a Small Island*. Still, the almost two years he spent working at Holloway were tremendously productive, if in an unexpected way. Dispatched one day to a new ward, he first saw "a pretty young nurse of clear and radiant goodness, caring for these helpless wrecks with boundless reserves of energy and compassion—guiding them to a chair, brightening their day with chatter, wiping dribble from their chins—and I thought, *This is just the sort of person I need*."

That student nurse was Cynthia Billen, and sixteen months later, after she had completed her training, she became Bryson's wife. The young couple honeymooned in Paris. "I had spent the whole of my savings," Bryson writes in *Neither Here nor There*, "some eighteen pounds, on a suit for the wedding—a remarkable piece of apparel with lapels that had been modeled on the tail fins of a 1957 Coupe de Ville and bell-bottom pants so copiously flared that when I walked, you didn't see my legs move." The honeymoon was financed by £12 (about $28 at that time) borrowed from Bryson's father-in-law, "in order, as I pointed out, to keep his daughter from starving during her first week of married life."

In 1975, the Brysons returned to America so that Bill could complete his bachelor of arts degree in political science at Drake. Thus, as he notes in *Thunderbolt Kid*, "Every bit of formal education I have ever had" took place in Des Moines. After finishing his degree, Bryson found that Britain still held him in thrall. In 1977 Bryson and his English wife returned to England, where they started a family and lived without interruption until 1995.

Living and Writing in England

The Brysons settled in Bournemouth, on the southern coast of England in Dorset. Bill took a job at the *Bournemouth Evening Echo*, the local newspaper, as a subeditor. (In Britain a subeditor is a copy editor—an editor in charge of making textual changes to a manuscript to ensure grammatical and factual accuracy and to make it conform to the publication's house style.) As he told the *Independent* in 2001, coming from a family of journalists, "it never really occurred to me to do anything else. All through my teenage years I assumed that I would one day be working on a newspaper."

After two years at Bournemouth, the Brysons moved to London, where Bill worked for *Financial Weekly* before joining the *Times* of London in 1981 as a subeditor. The *Times* is England's oldest daily newspaper (it was founded in 1785) and is considered the country's newspaper of record —a publication known for its professionalism and high journalistic standards. Bryson eventually became chief subeditor of the business section of the *Times*.

On October 7, 1986, a new British national newspaper, the *Independent*, was launched, with a left-leaning editorial slant that suited Bryson's political sensibilities. Bryson grew up, as he notes in *The Lost Continent*, in a family of Democrats, and in recent years he has described himself to the *Financial Times* as "considerably more left wing than your typical American Republican." Bryson became deputy national news editor of the business section of the *Independent*.

Meanwhile, the Brysons had started a family; they welcomed three children—a boy and then two girls—by the mid–1980s. "[T]o pay for washing machines and push-chairs," Bryson began writing freelance articles; his first piece was for *Sports Illustrated*. He wrote numerous travel articles for in-flight airline magazines, as well as pieces for the *New York Times, Washington Post, National Geographic, Granta,* and *GQ,* among others. Many of his early pieces were signed Bill Bryson Jr., "out of deference to his father." "Gradually I began to realise I enjoyed doing it and started to write a couple of small books in my spare time," he told the *Independent* in 2001.

His first two books (aside from *The Book of Blunders* [1982], a short collection of odd stories culled from years of reading the world press) were *The Penguin Dictionary of Troublesome Words* (1984; published simultaneously in the United States as *The Facts on File Dictionary of Troublesome Words*) and *The Palace under the Alps: And Over Two Hundred Other Unusual, Unspoiled, and Infrequently Visited Spots in Sixteen European Countries* (1985). The former is a guide for writers and editors, drawn from Bryson's own experience as a subeditor; the latter was inspired by his travel pieces. *The Palace under the Alps* is his only book published under the name William Bryson—a fact that Norman Oder attributes to the publisher "vainly seeking a veneer of class." While

The Palace under the Alps did not sell well (Bryson quipped that it was "instantly remaindered"), book contracts for *The Lost Continent* and *The Mother Tongue: English and How It Got That Way* soon followed. As Bryson told the *Independent* in 2001, the time had come to make a choice: "I quit my job as an assistant home editor at the *Independent* to take up writing full-time. It was a difficult decision. The thought of giving up a regular pay cheque was quite scary. I remember being appalled when I realised I wouldn't get paid for holidays any more."

The family moved to the Yorkshire Dales, in the north of England, and Cynthia gave birth to their fourth and final child, a son. Bryson called the move "a very big gamble" and noted that "in the first year I only made about £3,000. We had some money saved, but the six of us were basically living off Cynthia's wages as a nurse."

Loss and Success

The Brysons' circumstances changed when *The Lost Continent* was published in 1989. Upon the death of his father in 1986, Bryson was seized by the desire to revisit some of the family vacation spots that he had so dreaded as a child. So "one September dawn in my thirty-sixth year I crept out of my childhood home, slid behind the wheel of an aging Chevrolet Chevette lent me by my sainted and trusting mother, and guided it out through the flat, sleeping streets of the city."

Thirty-four days later, he was back in Des Moines, having driven 6,842 miles on a loop through the eastern

Bryson's interest in conservation was piqued when he and his family left London and moved to the countryside. In the Lake District, a wind farm is proposed to combat climate change.

United States that had taken him down to Mississippi, over to Georgia, up to Maine, across to both peninsulas of Michigan, and back down through Wisconsin to Iowa. After a similar loop through the western United States, Bryson notes, "I [had] visited all but ten of the lower forty-eight states and [driven] 13,978 miles." Bryson documented his travels with the sharp and often sarcastic wit that would become his trademark.

Bryson's rise to fame began with *The Lost Continent*, at least in Britain, where "its savage take on American tackiness made it a British hit." It was less popular in the United States, where Bryson's biting humor about his native land did not go over well. As Norman Oder notes, "some reviewers chided Bryson for cheap shots, like giving small towns such fictional names as 'Dry Heaves,' New Mexico." His next book, *The Mother Tongue*, a popular history of the English language, fared better in the United States.

While searching for a literary agent after the success of *The Lost Continent*, Bryson encountered a piece of good luck. A friend in New York, Bryson writes in *Thunderbolt Kid*, "mentioned a bright young man who had just quit the William Morris agency to set up on his own. 'His name's Jed Mattes,' he told me. 'You know, I think he might be from your hometown.'"

Indeed he was, and he and Bryson had been friends in Des Moines. Mattes plays the central role in a story in *Thunderbolt Kid*, and Bryson notes that he is "the only one of my contemporaries, I believe, to whom I have not given a pseudonym."

Mattes became Bryson's agent, and another book for Penguin followed in 1991. Essentially an expanded version of *The Penguin Dictionary of Troublesome Words*, *The Penguin Dictionary for Writers and Editors* covers a wider range of questions encountered by professional writers and those who prepare their words for print.

Bryson returned to travel writing with the publication of *Neither Here nor There: Travels in Europe* (1992). In the book Bryson comments on his absence from Europe since his two backpacking trips in 1972 and 1973: "I had spent almost the whole of my adulthood, fifteen of the last seventeen years, living in England, on the fringe of this glorious continent, and seen almost none of it." He decided "to put things right" by revisiting many of the places he had first seen during his earlier trips. The book skillfully and inventively weaves together the narrative of a grand tour through Europe of a man in midlife with a wife and four children with the hilarious reminiscences of the author's final months as a carefree, on-again, off-again college student, bouncing around Europe with the pseudonymous Stephen Katz.

For his next book Bryson returned to the subject of *The Mother Tongue* but with a twist. Rather than rehash the entire history of English, *Made in America: An Informal History of the English Language in the United States* (1994) details the contributions, for good and ill, that American speakers of English have made to the language. More than a mere examination of the history of American words, the book looks at the history of the United States through its language. The subjects covered include immigration, the rise of chain stores and shopping malls, the evolution of American politics, and the American fascination with technology. Along the way Bryson provides anecdotes illustrating historical examples of American wordplay, from the practice of Hollywood actors taking new names to the sources of famous American sayings, such as Theodore Roosevelt's "Speak softly and carry a big stick."

The Expat Is Repatriated

Around this time the Brysons began discussing another change in their lives, one that would be almost as momentous as Bill's decision to devote himself to writing full time. Despite their love for their home in the Yorkshire Dales, the remoteness of the location presented problems, particularly for Bryson's increasingly heavy travel schedule for research and book tours. "So we made the decision to move somewhere a little more urban and built-up," he writes in *I'm a Stranger Here Myself*. "And then—this is the part that gets hazy—somehow this simple concept evolved into the notion of settling in America for a time."

May 1995 found the Bryson family in Hanover, New Hampshire, the home of Dartmouth College. Before they left Britain, Bryson decided to take one final trip around his adopted homeland—and, of course, to turn the experience into a book. *Notes from a Small Island* (1995) is in some ways an unusual travel book, since it is less about discovering a new place than about saying goodbye to an old and familiar one. Yet just as in *Neither Here nor There*, Bryson interweaves a travel account (his seven-week trip in the fall of 1994) with reminiscences, this time of his two decades in Britain—starting once again by approaching England on the ferry from Calais. The result is as much memoir as travel book, and in this it anticipates *Thunderbolt Kid*, the more straightforward memoir of his early years that he wrote a decade later.

Notes from a Small Island was an immediate success; it sold more copies (2.2 million worldwide by 2007) than any of Bryson's previous books. The book was made into a two-part film for British television (it first aired in January 1999), and five years later, voters in the United Kingdom honored *Notes* by choosing it to receive the World Book Day award of 2003, as the book that best encapsulates the identity of contemporary Britain.

Having said his goodbyes to England (he planned to stay away for at least five years), Bryson notes in *I'm a Stranger Here Myself* his initial reaction to being back in America: "I can clearly recall . . . waking up in a strange house in New Hampshire, looking out the window, and thinking: 'What on earth am I doing here?'" In 2007 he told the *Guardian* that, as the five years stretched into eight, he spent his days "pining for Radio 4, the English sense of humour, and Branston pickle."

Yet his eight years as a repatriated expatriate were extraordinarily productive. Shortly after settling in New Hampshire, Bryson happened upon an entrance point to the Appalachian Trail in the woods on the edge of Hanover. For about seven months in 1996, he hiked 870 miles along the nearly 2,200-mile trail and reacquainted himself with the country of his birth. He was accompanied at the beginning and the end of his journey by Stephen Katz. The result was *A Walk in the Woods* (1998), Bryson's first travel book to achieve success on both sides of the Atlantic. It became a *New York Times* best seller and continued to sell briskly a decade later. (As of 2009, a film adaptation of the book, directed by Barry Levinson and starring Robert Redford as Bryson, has been announced as being in development for release in 2011.)

Just as he was drawing near the end of his hike, twenty-eight pounds lighter than when he began, Bryson received a phone call from a friend in London with the offer of a weekly column in the Sunday magazine of the London *Mail on Sunday*. From September 1996 to September 1998, Bryson wrote the columns on life in America that became *I'm a Stranger Here Myself* (1999; released in Britain as *Notes from a Big Country*).

From Down Under to Nearly Everything

Living in the United States did not dampen Bryson's enthusiasm for travel. As the 2000 Summer Olympic Games, scheduled to be held in Sydney, Australia, approached, Bryson got the idea for his next book. As Bryson noted, Australia was a country that remained something of an enigma even to Great Britain, its mother country, as well as to the rest of the English-speaking world. Bryson decided to do something about that, and so his 2000 book *In a Sunburned Country* (released in Britain with the title *Down Under*) was

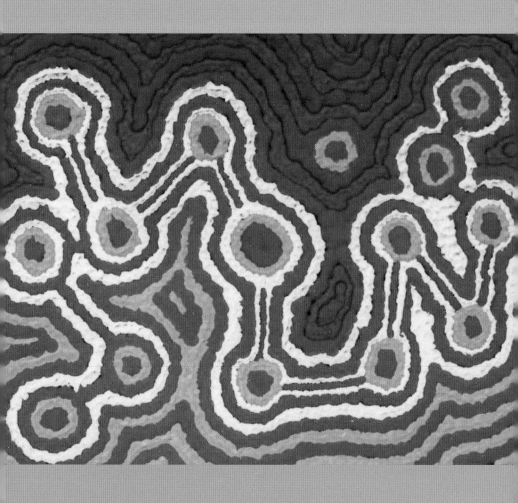

Bryson traveled to Australia for the 2000 Olympics. While there, he
learned more about the natural world and may have gotten to see
aboriginal art, such as this painting, "Helicopter Tjungurrayi," by
Pikarti Soak.

born. The book combined the travel writing that readers had come to expect with Bryson's increasing interest in the natural world (reflected also in *A Walk in the Woods*). Of all the continents, Australia is the oldest geologically and, as Bryson writes, "has more things that will kill you than anywhere else.... This is a country where even the fluffiest of caterpillars can lay you out with a toxic nip, where seashells will not just sting you but actually sometimes *go* for you." Because of the forbidding nature of the Outback and the relatively small population of the country (only 18 million at the time Bryson was writing), large portions of Australia are still relatively unknown.

Following up on the success of *In a Sunburned Country*, Bryson returned to the pages of his old employer, the London *Times*, as a columnist during the Sydney Olympics.

While returning from a trip to Australia in the late 1990s, Bryson conceived the notion for the book that would take the longest time for him to research and to write but would also result in the highest sales of his career. *A Short History of Nearly Everything* (2003) may not seem particularly short (with notes, it weighs in at over 500 pages); however, it covers somewhere around 13.7 billion years, from the dawn of the universe to the present day, and provides the reader with at least a passing acquaintance with all of the major scientific disciplines.

As Bryson cheerfully admitted, when he began his three years of research for *A Short History of Nearly Everything*, "I didn't know what a proton was, or a protein, didn't know a quark from a quasar." Moreover, in discussing certain modern scientific controversies (such as whether modern man, *Homo sapiens*, displaced all premodern men or whether the latter disappeared through absorption into the modern gene pool), he had to navigate rather heated debates. Yet despite these odds, *A Short History* garnered nearly universal praise for its ability to make even such complicated concepts as Einstein's theory of relativity and Heisenberg's uncertainty principle accessible to the average reader.

In 2004 *A Short History* won the prestigious Aventis Prize for science writing. (Bryson donated the £10,000 in prize money to the Great Ormond Street Hospital Children's Charity.) A year later Bryson was honored with the Descartes Prize for Science Communication, awarded by the European Union. In 2006 Bryson donated some of the royalties from *A Short History* to help the Royal Society of Chemistry establish the RSC Bill Bryson Prize, an essay competition for primary- and secondary-school students.

By May 2007 this engagingly written examination of the current state of scientific knowledge (and of how that state was arrived at) had sold 2.7 million copies worldwide. Bryson produced a rewritten version of the book for younger readers in 2008, entitled *A Really Short History of Nearly Everything*.

As he was completing his research for *A Short History*, Bryson was asked by the aid agency CARE International to visit its operations in Africa and to document his experience in a book. *Bill Bryson's African Diary* (2002) is the shortest of Bryson's works, no more than an extended essay covering eight days in Kenya. It is also his least humorous work, a point that Bryson freely admits. As Simon Hattenstone wrote in a profile of Bryson for the *Guardian*, "He's just been to Kenya, and he's got to write a little book about it, and nothing funny happened." What emerges instead is an intimate portrait of human suffering and of those who dedicate years—or even their entire lives—thousands of miles from home to alleviating it. Both Bryson and his publisher, Broadway Books, donated all of the proceeds from the book to CARE.

A decade and a half after Bryson began to devote himself to writing full time, he had "become a brand." *The Penguin Dictionary of Troublesome Words* was released in an updated edition in 2002 as *Bryson's Dictionary of Troublesome Words*. New paperback editions of older works were released; the paperback edition of *The Lost Continent* enjoyed the success in the United States that it had failed to attain the first time around.

Back to England

After eight years in New Hampshire, in mid–2003 the Brysons returned to England—this time, it seems, permanently. While living in the United States in 1998, Bryson told Norman Oder of *Publishers Weekly* that he felt torn between his native land and his adopted country. "With every passing month, it becomes harder. I'm definitely an American, because I grew up here. But I've lived very happily in Britain." In that same vein, Oder and other interviewers have commented on Bryson's "not-quite-British accent," which sounds British to American ears, but more American to British ones.

In December 2003, five months after returning to England, Bryson told an interviewer from the *Financial Times* that he had "no urge" to return to the United States, other than to visit his elderly mother in Iowa. In 2005 Bryson began the process of obtaining British citizenship; he humorously suggested to the *Guardian* that "they'll probably turn me down." (As of 2009 Bryson remained an American citizen.)

The Brysons settled near Wymondham, Norfolk (which, Bryson notes in *The Mother Tongue*, is pronounced "wind-hum"), where they took up residence in a nineteenth-century rectory. "Every morning of my life now I wake up in a house in Norfolk and look out a bedroom window at a church tower that was built in the time of the Normans. It has been there for 900 years. I find that a literally fantastic statement. For anyone from a young country, that depth of built heritage is just dazzling."

Bryson's fascination with the historic architecture of England is one reason why, after returning to England in 2003, he was appointed a commissioner for English Heritage, a UK government organization similar to the National Trust for Historic Preservation in the United States. English Heritage oversees historic archaeological and architectural sites—among them Holloway Sanatorium, where Bryson and his wife first met. After undergoing a six-year art restoration and conversion process between 1994 and 2000, Holloway Sanatorium is now a gated housing development. In *Notes from a Small Island*, Bryson describes some of the changes that preserved "probably one of the dozen finest Victorian structures still standing" from destruction.

Bryson wrote glowingly in *Notes from a Small Island* of Durham, a "perfect little city" in the northeast of England, which he visited on impulse during his farewell tour in 1994 "and fell in love with it instantly in a serious way." On April 4, 2005, Bryson was appointed chancellor of Durham University (he succeeded the late actor and director Peter Ustinov). The appointment was something of an ironic development for the man who attended kindergarten only when he felt like it and who took seven years to get his undergraduate degree. The *Guardian* called Bryson "the accidental chancellor," and Bryson himself said, "I can't quite believe the university asked me." Although the chancellorship (the equivalent of a college presidency in the United States) "can vary from the figurehead that breezes in for a few days a year to the rather more hands-on," Bryson took a very active role after taking the reins. (Bryson had received an honorary doctorate in civil law from Durham University in 2004.)

The period after Bryson's return to England marked the longest gap between the publication of major works since he became a full-time writer. In 2006 *The Life and Times of the Thunderbolt Kid*, a memoir of growing up in Des Moines, appeared, and the sales reflected pent-up demand. In honor of the book's publication, the mayor of Des Moines proclaimed October 21, 2006, Bill Bryson "The Thunderbolt Kid" Day and presented Bryson the key to the city. The official proclamation notes that "Bill's razor-sharp wit gently impales our midwestern need for nostalgia, no matter how mundane, and makes us see ourselves in a new light" and adds, perhaps playfully, that "Bill has put Des Moines, for better or worse, in the minds of millions of his fans."

Two months later, Bryson received yet another high honor—indeed, the highest honor that Great Britain can give to a noncitizen. On December 13 Bryson was raised to honorary membership in the Order of the British Empire for his contributions to literature. The culture secretary Tessa Jowell, presenting the honor, declared, "Despite having been born and raised in the US, [Bryson] has become a true British institution." For the 2006–2007 academic year, Bryson was named Schwartz Visiting Fellow of the Pomfret School, an elite coeducational academy in Connecticut, and later that year he received the James Joyce Award of the Literary and Historical Society of University College Dublin. (The Literary and Historical Society was founded by John Henry Newman, the author of *The Idea of the University*. Cardinal Newman [1801–1890], one of Britain's most esteemed writers, was a famous convert from Anglicanism to Roman Catholicism.)

Thunderbolt Kid was followed in 2007 by *Shakespeare: The World as Stage*. This short biography of William Shakespeare eschews the speculation that is central to so many works on the poet and playwright and offers instead a "just the facts" approach. As Bryson points out, Shakespeare "is at once the best known and least known of figures," and much of what is known about him simply deepens the mystery surrounding his life. Other authors often make up for the lack of historical details about Shakespeare by creating theories about the playwright. "Even the most careful biographers sometimes take a supposition—that Shakespeare was Catholic or happily married or fond of the countryside or kindly disposed toward animals—and convert it within a page or two to something like a certainty." To avoid this temptation, Bryson turns his eye outward and places those facts that are known about Shakespeare within the context of his times. He thus teases out a more complete picture of Shakespeare's life from the details of the lives of his contemporaries.

Environmental Activism

The small towns and countryside of England were what first attracted Bryson to the island, as he documented lovingly and humorously in *Notes from a Small Island*. Concern over the increasing destruction of open spaces and the changing nature of English small towns and villages led him to accept the presidency of the Campaign to Protect Rural England (CPRE) in May 2007. CPRE is one of the oldest environmental groups in the world, and its primary concern since its founding in 1926 has been to limit urban sprawl, a particular problem in England's island environment. Within days the chief executive of CPRE told the *Guardian*, "We've already had a membership surge since the news got out" that Bryson would become president.

Bryson once again threw himself into a new role—as he had when he was named chancellor of Durham University. He decided to put CPRE's expanded membership to good use. In April 2008 he announced the start of a campaign, Stop the Drop, that sought to halt the epidemic of littering in Great Britain. It was a problem that had frequently come up during discussions on his book tours around England and that he had noted as far back as 1995 in *Notes from a*

In April 2008, Bryson teamed up with the Wombles, "green" British TV puppets, to launch an antilitter campaign called "Stop the Drop." Bryson had become president of the Campaign to Protect Rural England the previous year.

Small Island: "I took a train to Liverpool. They were having a festival of litter when I arrived. Citizens had taken time off from their busy activities to add ice cream wrappers, empty cigarette boxes, and plastic carrier bags to the otherwise bland and neglected landscape." While the antilitter campaign is primarily voluntary, Bryson favors government actions to force people to dispose of their trash properly. "We are not asking you to do anything but keep it with you until you get out [of] the car and then put it in the bin. If you're so idle and cretinous you can't even do that, then someone has to force you to do it," he told *Marketing* magazine in April 2008. He has supported legislation mandating a deposit on bottles and cans, a solution that has long been used effectively in the United States. On August 11, 2008, *Panorama*, a long-running television program on BBC One, aired an episode entitled "Notes on a Dirty Island," in which Bryson graphically illustrated the problem of litter and presented some success stories—including Liverpool, which has cleaned up its streets in recent years.

Bryson has continued to support the traditional goals of CPRE as well. In November 2008 he criticized plans to create a 10,000-home "eco-town" in the Norfolk countryside and proposed instead that existing towns be made "eco-friendly." "There is a lot to be said for existing towns which give people a sense of history and a sense of place," he told an online news service in Norwich, Evening News 24. "Most could absorb more people."

Bryson's remarks echo a theme that runs through all of his books—travel books, memoirs, histories of language, and even his study of science. The countryside exists for humankind, but cities and towns must, too. Travel is meaningless without the traveler, as is language when separated from those who speak and write it. Even if human existence is a fluke, a position that Bryson does not rule out, the history of science remains fascinating because human beings are here, and that, as Bryson puts it in *A Short History of Nearly Everything*, "has required a nearly endless string of good fortune."

Nearing the end of his sixth decade of life, Bryson shows no sign of slowing down, though he is increasingly aware of the passage of time: "I have a finite amount of time left." His wife, he has said for years, "would very much prefer it if I did a book where I stayed at home," and he seems now to agree: "I want to be home for dinner. The one downside of my career has been all the time I've been away from home, particularly with the travel books."

His wish to stay at home may mean that readers will see more books like *Shakespeare: The World as Stage* and *A Short History of Nearly Everything,* which required less travel, and fewer like *A Walk in the Woods,* which required him to be away from home for a lengthy period. Bryson is unlikely to set aside his keyboard anytime soon, though. As he told an interviewer in January 2007, "a writer's life is such a pleasure. People pay you to go to interesting places and meet interesting people. I don't have to iron a shirt in the morning or put on a tie. The freedom is so wonderful."

When the United States dropped atomic bombs on Hiroshima and
Nagasaki, it ended World War II. America emerged as the undisputed
leader of the postwar world.

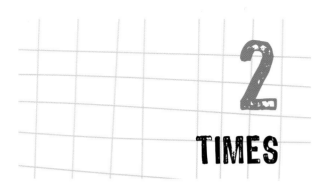

TIMES

A DECADE BEFORE BILL BRYSON was born, Henry Luce, the cofounder and publisher of *Time* magazine, wrote an editorial for *Life* magazine, another of his publications. Entitled "The American Century," the February 17, 1941, editorial summed up a sense of optimism shared by many Americans as the country began to climb out of the depths of the Great Depression. Europe and Asia were torn by war, but the United States was still ten months away from the Japanese attack on Pearl Harbor and its subsequent entry into World War II.

In the face of the competing despotisms of Nazi Germany and Soviet Russia and Imperial Japan's dominance over the Far East, Luce offered an alternative American vision of a world united not by "Tyranny" but by "Freedom," "Justice," and "Peace." (Luce capitalized these and other key terms throughout the editorial.)

"Tyrannies," Luce wrote, "may require a large amount of living space. But Freedom requires and will require far greater living space than Tyranny. Peace cannot endure unless it prevails over a very large part of the world. Justice will come near to losing all meaning in the minds of men unless Justice can have approximately the same fundamental meanings in many lands and among many peoples." Only America, in Luce's opinion, could offer a vision of international order that would ensure freedom, justice, and peace for the world.

American internationalism, Luce wrote, "cannot come out of the vision of any one man. It must be the product of the imagination of many men. It must be a sharing with all peoples of our Bill of Rights, our Declaration of Independence, our Constitution, our magnificent industrial products, our technical skills." Paraphrasing Abraham Lincoln's Gettysburg Address, Luce declared, "It must be an internationalism of the people, by the people and for the people."

A New and Confident America

Four and a half years later the United States dropped atomic bombs on the Japanese cities of Hiroshima and Nagasaki, and the destruction of World War II came to an end. America emerged as the undisputed leader of the postwar world; the Soviet Union, weakened by the war, did not mount a serious challenge to American dominance for several more years. To many it seemed that Luce's vision was on its way to becoming reality: the twentieth century became popularly known as the American Century.

American life in the 1950s, as Bill Bryson noted in *The Life and Times of the Thunderbolt Kid*, was marked by an optimism perhaps never before seen and certainly never seen since. American manufacturing, which had been spurred on

Comic books and science fiction became very popular with kids in the 1950s. In this photo from 1959, a boy wearing a futuristic space helmet and goggles demonstrates Robbie the Robot: it walks, it talks, and its eyes light up, all by remote control.

to new heights by the need to make weapons and vehicles for World War II, was now converted to peacetime use. The public developed a fascination with science and technology, and magazines such as *Popular Mechanics* and *Popular Science*, both decades old, gained a new generation of avid subscribers. War movies and Western films increasingly gave way to science fiction. Had he been born a decade earlier, Bryson might have adopted the persona of a cowboy or frontiersman as a child; instead, even though (as he writes in *Thunderbolt Kid*), "On my head, according to season, I wore a green felt cowboy hat or a Davy Crockett coonskin cap," Bryson's childhood fantasy was to be a science-fiction superhero from another galaxy, the Thunderbolt Kid.

From Farm to City, from City to Suburb

Starting in the late nineteenth century and accelerated first by the Great Depression and then by World War II, a shift in the American population from the countryside to the city had taken place. Mass production made tractors and other farming implements more affordable; farm machinery, in turn, decreased the need for manual farm labor. Bryson's paternal grandparents lived in a small farming community in southeastern Iowa; his maternal grandfather worked in the stockyards of Nebraska. His parents, though, had moved to Des Moines, the capital of and largest city in Iowa: his mother, to study journalism at Drake University; his father, to work for the *Des Moines Register*. Bryson and his older brother and sister, like many young people of mid-twentieth-century

America, knew the countryside largely as a place to visit.

As public transportation, especially streetcars, developed in the early part of the century, the population of large cities such as New York and Los Angeles began to spread outward into the suburbs. Such suburbs, however, were different from modern-day suburbs; they were essentially extensions of urban development rather than self-contained developments.

In the wake of World War II, however, another population shift occurred. Starting in the 1940s city dwellers on the east and west coasts began to move into modern self-contained suburban developments; by the late 1950s the trend spread to the midwest. Suburban houses featured new technology; kitchens, in particular, received the fruits of American industry. Refrigerators, electric stoves and ovens —and, a little later, dishwashers and microwaves—became commonplace. In the process these labor-saving devices, along with new techniques for preserving and packaging food that made mass production possible (flash-freezing, for example), freed up the time of housewives. For the first time, not only in American history but in the history of the world, the stage was set for large numbers of women to be employed outside the home.

From Kitchen to Office

Single women (meaning largely women who had never married, since, until almost 1970, the divorce rate was still relatively low in the United States; 13.4 per thousand married women in 1969 *versus* 22.8 per thousand at its peak a decade

In the wake of World War II, middle-class families migrated en masse to the suburbs.

Bill Bryson's mother was part of another wave: the dramatic increase of women in the workforce that started during the 1950s.

later) had long participated in the workforce at high levels. Between 1950 and 1985, the percentage of single women between the ages of twenty-five and forty-four who were employed outside of the home hovered around 80 percent. George Gilder noted in the September 1986 *Atlantic* that the workforce of married women in that age group had increased—"from 26 percent in 1950 to some 67 percent in the mid–1980s"—though most were still employed only in part-time or seasonal work.

The increase of young mothers in the workforce was even more dramatic; Bill Bryson's mother, Mary, was one of them. "At the end of the Second World War," wrote Gilder, "only 10 percent of married women with children under the age of six held jobs or were seeking them." The next forty years saw a sea change in that figure: "By 1985 the census had classified more than half of these young mothers as participants in the work force."

The U.S. Department of Labor noted that, as of 2007, "women comprised 46% of the total U.S. labor force." Moreover, "a record 68 million women were employed in the U.S.," and most—75 percent—were employed full time. Thirty-nine percent of women in the workforce were employed in "management, professional, and related occupations"; furthermore, "women accounted for 51% of all workers in the high-paying management, professional, and related occupations." In *Thunderbolt Kid*, Bryson writes that, regarding women in the workforce, "my father was commendably—I would even say enthusiastically—liberal, for there was nothing about my mother's earning capacity that didn't gladden his heart." Still, even the senior Bill Bryson could not have predicted such a marked change in the workforce in 1950.

This dramatic and seemingly permanent demographic shift in the workforce, coming at the same time that technology was bringing about an unprecedented rise in productivity, had a profound effect on the U.S. economy. As Bryson notes in *Thunderbolt Kid*, "The economy had become an unstoppable machine: gross national product rose by 40 percent in the decade, from about $350 billion in 1950 to nearly $500 billion ten years later, then rose by another third to $658 billion in the next six years." (Gross domestic product in 2008 was $14.2 trillion.) "People were wealthier than ever before," Bryson writes, "but life somehow didn't seem as much fun."

The entrance of women into the workforce was made possible in part by labor-saving devices, but working women also fed the market for such appliances and gadgets. "Women increasingly went out to work"—or converted from part-time work to full-time employment—"to help keep the whole enterprise afloat. Soon millions of people were caught in a spiral in which they worked harder and harder to buy labor-saving devices that they wouldn't have needed if they hadn't been working so hard in the first place."

Spending Grows, Families Shrink

More families found themselves drawn into this spiral by another innovation of the 1950s. Individual stores had long offered customers charge accounts, and in the 1920s, some of those stores had introduced charge cards to make charging an item to an account easier. But the Diners Club card, created in 1950, was the first charge card that could be used at more than one business; it was followed by the American Express card in 1958. Charge cards required that the full balance be paid each month, but 1958 also saw the introduction of the BankAmericard (which eventually became Visa), the first national credit card. Charge cards and credit cards made it easier to purchase goods even when the family income was not rising as fast as expenditures. Both could be used instead of cash, and unlike checks, neither required the buyer to have funds in the bank to cover the purchase. Unlike charge cards, however, credit cards allowed the holder to maintain a balance, so long as he or she paid a portion of it each month. Personal credit, largely restricted in the past to mortgages and car loans, now helped to finance increased consumption.

While spending was on the rise, average family size in the United States, which had remained relatively stable during the first two decades of the 1900s, had been on the decline since 1920, as families moved from rural areas, where the manual labor of children was more valued, to urban ones. The postwar baby boom (from 1946 to 1964) reversed that trend for a while. During the decade of the 1950s, the central part of the baby boom, family size rose slightly, from 3.0 in 1950 to 3.1 in 1960. In 1950, 58.2 percent of families had children under eighteen living at home; in 1960, 60.6 percent.

Average family size declined markedly after 1960; it hit 2.5 in the years 2002–2003. In a footnote in *Thunderbolt Kid*,

Bryson wryly notes, "Altogether the mothers of post-war America gave birth to 76 million kids between 1946 and 1964, when their poor old overworked wombs all gave out more or less at once, evidently." Decreases in infant mortality through medical advances were more than offset by lower birthrates—a dramatic cultural shift. The median age of Americans rose from 29.5 (1960) to 35.3 (2002–2003). Bryson's "Kid World" of mid-twentieth-century America had grown up.

Furthermore, those grown-ups were going places. In 1950, "59 percent of households owned an auto"; a decade later, the number had risen to 73 percent. By 1970, "80.1 percent of U.S. families owned at least one" car, and it had become common for two-earner families to own two. By the years 2002–2003, "there was at least one vehicle in 88 percent of U.S. households, with the average family owning 2.0."

Rising wages led to greater disposable income that could be spent on automobiles (and their maintenance and fuel), and greater female participation in the workforce fueled the need for multiple cars in a family. American mobility was also helped along by government actions. Bryson notes in *Made in America* that the American streetcar system had peaked in 1922, with "over fourteen thousand miles of streetcar track," but even before World War II, public resources shifted from mass transportation to roads.

The Age of the Highway

"In 1923 the Lincoln Highway—the first transcontinental highway in the world—officially opened." It stretched from

New York to San Francisco. "For the next forty years, it hummed with life as a daily cavalcade of cars and trucks brought commerce and the intoxicating whiff of a larger, livelier world to the hundreds of little towns (it mostly avoided cities) standing along its pleasantly meandering route." The Lincoln Highway had been an interesting partnership between private donors and local and state governments, but shortly thereafter, the federal government began to devote its attention to the construction of highways.

The largest federal road project in history officially began when, at the request of President Dwight D. Eisenhower, Congress passed the Federal-Aid Highway Act of 1956 (commonly known as the National Interstate and Defense Highways Act). As Bryson notes in *Made in America*, the act had its roots in an event that took place almost four decades earlier: "In 1919, the U.S. Army sent a convoy of trucks cross-country from Camp Meade, Maryland, to San Francisco, just to see if it could be done. It could, but only just. The trip took two months at an average speed of less than seven miles an hour. The young officer in charge of the convoy was Dwight D. Eisenhower."

The National Interstate and Defense Highways Act set aside $25 billion to build the Interstate Highway System over a period of twelve years. The initial construction ended in 1992, thirty-five years after the project began, and cost $114.3 billion in federal funds. The system continues to grow: as of 2004 the Interstate Highway System included nearly 47,000 miles of roads.

The Interstate Highway System turned the American

fascination with automobiles into a full-blown love affair. By the 1960s the cross-country family vacations that play a central role in Bryson's memories of his childhood (in *Thunderbolt Kid*, for instance) had become commonplace. Bryson's first commercially successful book, *The Lost Continent*, recalls the days when both white- and blue-collar families took off for a week or two during the summer and drove to some distant point, where they spent a few days relaxing and then drove back home again. For the book Bryson revisited all of the places that his father had taken the family (as well as other popular tourist destinations from the middle decades of the twentieth century). The distance he covered—almost 14,000 miles—provides some sense of the centrality of the automobile to American leisure in the 1960s.

Chain Stores and Supermarkets

The rise of what was known as the "car culture" in the United States had far-reaching ramifications. As Bryson notes in *Made in America*, "In the early 1930s, a survey of the highway between New York and New Haven revealed that there was on average a gas station every 895 feet and a restaurant or diner every 1,825 feet." Hundreds of miles from home, travelers had no sure way of judging the quality of local restaurants or motels. By the mid–1950s they increasingly relied on chains, such as Howard Johnson's and Holiday Inn, which provided a standard experience when the traveler from Des Moines found himself in such diverse places as Washington, D.C., and Anaheim, California.

The success of chain restaurants and other businesses

that arose from the car culture, combined with the increasing ease of transporting goods from coast to coast provided by the growing Interstate Highway System, spurred on the adoption of the chain model by such traditionally local enterprises as grocery and department stores. A number of national chains had been around for some time, including J. C. Penney, which had a total of 1,600 stores across all forty-eight states by 1941, and F. W. Woolworth Company, the first "five and dime" store, which had opened in 1879. More followed the path of Younkers, the largest department store in Des Moines and the one that plays a central role in Bryson's childhood memories in *Thunderbolt Kid*. Younkers began as a statewide chain in the 1920s; in the 1950s it expanded outside of Iowa and eventually had stores throughout the midwest.

"As late as 1955," Bryson writes in *Made in America*, "95 percent of America's 360,000 grocery stores were mom-and-pop corner businesses or medium-sized stores known as *superettes*." The writing was on the wall, however: "Although supermarkets accounted for just 5 percent of grocery outlets, they already had half of America's food sales." The growth was just beginning. Founded in 1962, the most successful chain ever, Walmart, had over 4,100 stores in the United States by 2009, with sales of $401 billion worldwide. One of the secrets to Walmart's success has been its strategy of using its vast fleet of trucks as a "warehouse on wheels"; Walmart keeps storage costs low by using the Interstate Highway System in place of warehouses.

Chain stores offered convenience combined with lower prices than most locally owned stores. While they may seem

Among Bryson's laments are the homogenization of modern society brought on in no small part by huge discount chains such as Walmart.

a largely American phenomenon, the model (and sometimes the chains themselves, in the case of Woolworth's and, later, Walmart) began to spread around the world. One of the recurring themes of Bryson's *Notes from a Small Island* is the homogenization of life in Britain—brought on, in part, by economic centralization. Of Aberdeen, Scotland, he notes, "I could get exactly the same things, the same shops, libraries, and leisure centers, the same pubs and television programs, the same phone boxes, post offices, traffic lights, park benches, zebra crossings, marine air, and post-Indian-dinner burps, anywhere else." The success of this homogenization is explained by the very elements that make it not entirely satisfying: "In an odd way the very things that had made Aberdeen seem so dull and predictable the night before now made it feel comfortable and homey."

Urban Renewal, Urban Blight

Homogenization was driven not only by economic centralization but by the redesigning of cities in both the United States and Britain, a process known in America as urban renewal and in Britain as urban regeneration. As people moved from cities to the suburbs, portions of cities—often the downtown areas or the oldest, most historically important sections—fell into disrepair. Like suburbanization, the pro-cess began in the United States first on the east and west coasts and only later came to the midwest. (It is absent from Bryson's discussion of his childhood in *Thunderbolt Kid*; it appears only in retrospect, as he looks back from the vantage point of the twenty-first century.)

In 1949 Congress passed the Housing Act, which provided federal funds to cities to purchase private residences and businesses in areas deemed "slums" and to raze them. New, "modern" buildings were erected in their place. Five years later the Housing Act of 1954 provided federally backed mortgages to developers to make rebuilding more attractive. In the wake of the National Interstate and Defense Highways Act of 1956, federal highway funds were used to bring interstate highways into the centers of cities; the result often was destruction not only of blighted areas but of still-vibrant neighborhoods. "Soon every city had to have a freeway of its own," writes Bryson in *Made in America*, "even if it meant scything through old neighborhoods, as with Boston's destructive Downtown Artery, or slicing into a beauty spot like Fairmount Park with the Schuylkill (popularly known as the 'Sure-Kill') Expressway in Philadelphia."

Over the course of a quarter of a century, many historic buildings and even entire neighborhoods were replaced with modern structures. In the final chapter of *Thunderbolt Kid*, Bryson details some of the loss in Des Moines, including the Des Moines Theater, "not just the finest theater in the city but possibly the finest surviving theater of any type between Chicago and the West Coast." (It was replaced by a modern office building.) "My peerless Little League park, with its grandstand and press box, was torn down so that somebody could build an enormous apartment building in its place."

As striking as these examples of urban renewal in America are, they pale next to those Bryson offers in *Notes from a Small Island*. Urban regeneration in Britain involved the destruction of much older buildings and neighborhoods, many of them of historical significance, and the new structures provided an even greater contrast with fifteenth- and sixteenth-century British buildings than with nineteenth- and early-twentieth-century American ones. As a child Bryson had watched a famous film entitled *This Is Cinerama*, which was supposed to represent the future of the motion-picture industry. (In contrast to the small, boxy, black-and-white screen of 1950s television, *This Is Cinerama* was presented in vibrant color on a wide screen that curved at the edges so that the theater patron's entire field of view was engaged.) One of the segments of the movie, filmed in 1951, included a view of Princes Street in Edinburgh, Scotland, shot from Edinburgh Castle, high above the city.

In *Notes from a Small Island*, Bryson writes about viewing *This Is Cinerama* again in Bradford, England, during his 1994 trip around Britain. Having seen the shot of Princes Street, he was able to assess the change when he arrived in Edinburgh a short time later. "In 1951, Princes Street remained one of the world's great streets, a gracious thoroughfare lined along its northern side with solid, weighty Victorian and Edwardian edifices that bespoke confidence, greatness, and empire: the North British Mercantile Insurance Company, the sumptuous, classical New Club building, the old Waverley Hotel. And then, one by one, they were unaccountably torn down, and replaced for the most part with gray concrete bunkers." Throughout Britain (and in America), city centers were bulldozed to put up modern shopping malls.

As Bryson notes in *Made in America*, the results were the

same when the shopping malls were placed on empty land on the outskirts of towns and cities. "As shopping centers blossomed, downtowns began to die. Between 1948 and 1954, at the height of America's postwar economic boom, downtown retailers in America's thirteen largest cities lost on average a quarter of their business. One by one, downtowns grew more lifeless as stores and offices fled to the suburbs. Hudson's Department Store in Detroit closed after watching its annual sales fall from $153 million in 1953 to $45 million in 1981, its last year—the victim, ironically, of the automobile, the product that had brought Detroit its wealth."

Paying the Toll

By the time Bryson first settled in England, in 1973, the cycle of getting and spending was beginning to take its toll on the worldwide economy. The U.S. economy peaked in the final quarter of 1973 and entered a sixteen-month recession, the effects of which were felt across the globe. Inflation—an increase in the prices of goods and services and a consequent fall in the purchasing power of money—hit 6.8 percent in the first three quarters of 1973. Adjusted for inflation, average household income in the United States began a decline that lasted until the mid–1980s. Average household income did not recover to 1973 levels until the early years of the twenty-first century—a recovery that was due in part to an increase in the average number of hours worked per household (an increase largely attributable to the increased participation of wives and mothers in the workforce).

A series of economic recessions in the 1970s and early 1980s, before inflation was brought under control, wreaked further havoc on American and British cities. Manufacturing was especially hard hit, and much of the American midwest—known as the Rust Belt, because of its reliance on industry—saw double-digit unemployment. In Britain, too, areas that relied on manufacturing were disproportionately affected. As Bryson writes in *Notes from a Small Island*, if Britain were divided into "two halves with roughly 27 million people on each side," the northern half would rely more heavily on industry than the southern half. "Between 1980 and 1985, the southern half lost 103,600 jobs. The northern half in the same period lost 1,032,000, almost exactly ten times as many. And still the factories are shutting." (The Yorkshire Dales, where Bryson and his family lived until 1995, falls into that northern half.)

Thatcher and Reagan

One result of the economic uncertainty, in both the United States and Britain, was a change in the political climate. With the Democratic Party in control in the United States and the Labour Party holding Parliament in Britain, voters turned to more conservative political candidates and parties. In May 1979 the Conservative Party in Britain, having campaigned on economic issues (including controlling inflation and lowering taxes), won control of Parliament, and Margaret Thatcher became prime minister. She held the office until November 1990.

In November 1980 Ronald Reagan, the candidate of the Republican Party, won the U.S. presidency in a landslide. In both the United States and Britain, the 1980s were characterized by an emphasis on economic growth, including the lowering of personal and corporate income taxes and deregulation of industry. In Britain many state-owned industries, including national utilities and shipyards, were privatized, and public housing units were sold to tenants.

Both President Reagan and Prime Minister Thatcher had campaigned against the postwar welfare states in their respective countries, but Thatcher, dubbed the Iron Lady for her strength of will, was more successful in carrying through on her promises. She fought to reduce the power of trade unions, particularly those that represented government workers. Her actions encouraged private employers to do the same, including the Australian-born media mogul Rupert Murdoch, whose News International corporation had purchased the *Times* of London in 1981, a few months after Bryson began working there.

The British national press is often referred to as Fleet Street, after the street in London where the printing trade first developed and where most of the national newspapers were based until the late 1980s. "To say that Fleet Street in the early 1980s was out of control barely hints at the scale of matters," writes Bryson in *Notes from a Small Island*. The printers' union held such power that "many senior printers, with skills no more advanced than you would expect to find in any back-street print shop, enjoyed incomes in the top 2 percent of British earnings. It was crazy and clearly unsustainable."

That period came to an end on January 24, 1986, when the printers' union went on strike against News International. With the support of the Thatcher administration, "the *Times* abruptly sacked 5,250 members of the most truculent unions." The newspaper was moved to a new plant in

Wapping, in the East End of London, which Murdoch had secretly prepared in anticipation of a strike. There, the fired union members mounted demonstrations for over a year before giving in. By 1988 most of the other major British newspapers had dismissed their print union employees and left Fleet Street; the last newspaper left in August 1989.

The End of the American Century

With the fall of the Berlin Wall in 1989 and the collapse of the Soviet Union two years later, it seemed that the twentieth century had indeed been the American Century. Pundits began to ask whether the twenty-first century might be a second American Century. America was the world's only undisputed superpower; American-style capitalism appeared to have triumphed over Soviet communism and Western-European-style socialism. When the Democratic Party recaptured the U.S. presidency in 1992 and the Labour Party in Britain took Parliament in 1997, both continued many of the economic policies established by Reagan and Thatcher.

Bryson, whose parents had been Democrats, wrote critically of both Thatcher and Reagan (and even more critically of the effects of their policies). When his family moved to New Hampshire in May 1995, Bill Clinton was president, yet Bryson was critical of him as well. He told the *Guardian* in 2002, a few months before his family returned to Britain, that "Clinton's performance as president is one of the greatest disappointments in his life—here was a man with the ability to do the job and he blew it." Obliquely referring to the scandal that resulted in President Clinton's impeachment in 1998, Bryson remarked, "I am not a terribly moralistic person, but I do think in certain circumstances you are a model, and that you have to adhere to certain measures of decorum—at least extreme discretion, you know. And I think Clinton failed miserably on that score."

In that same interview Bryson commented on Clinton's Republican successor, George W. Bush. He "may be a more decent, reliable human being at that kind of level, but his shortcomings are other." The eight years of the Bush administration were marked by the so-called War on Terror, a response to the destruction by Islamic militants of the World Trade Center in New York City and a similar attack on the Pentagon on September 11, 2001. The War on Terror included actual wars in Afghanistan, starting in late 2001, and Iraq, launched in March 2003. Economically and militarily, the United States remained the world's major superpower, but a resurgent post-communist Russia began to challenge U.S. hegemony over Europe. In Britain, the Labour prime minister, Tony Blair, had supported the U.S. war in Iraq, but among the British population and throughout Europe, the war became increasingly unpopular, as it did in the United States.

Bryson opposed the war in Iraq, and the *Guardian* noted in 2005 that there were rumors that he and his family had returned to Britain because of it. "Not so," he told the *Guardian*, "though obviously it is a great comfort to know there is a whole ocean between George Bush and me." Noting that he had begun the process of obtaining British citizenship and referring to the controversial detention by the Bush administration of suspected Islamic terrorists at an

American naval base in Cuba, Bryson joked, "I'm a little worried that when I do this [formally renounce his U.S. citizenship] they'll pack me off to Guantanamo."

In the final months of 2008, the American economy entered a severe recession that some economists began to compare with the Great Depression. Congress passed a $700 billion plan to bail out banks and other financial institutions that had overextended credit to American consumers and home buyers. The Federal Reserve and the U.S. Treasury intervened as well; all told, bailout funds extended into the trillions of dollars. The stock market fell to levels it had first reached in 1997, and American manufacturing, the economic engine that Henry Luce had believed would drive America to dominate the world, sank to its lowest depths since World War II. Hit by collapsing credit markets, auto manufacturers, both domestic and foreign, saw U.S. sales drop by as much as 40 percent, and both the outgoing Bush administration and the administration of President Barack Obama extended loans to domestic car companies in an attempt to stave off bankruptcy. Still, General Motors, the world's largest automobile company from 1931 to 2008 and the one most closely identified with the "car culture" of the twentieth century, filed for bankruptcy protection on June 1, 2009. Few people now were suggesting that the United States might be entering a second American Century.

The world had become a much different place from the one in which the Thunderbolt Kid grew up.

A *Walk in the Woods* is arguably Bill Bryson's best-known book. The idea for it came from—a walk in the woods.

WORKS

A Walk in the Woods

IN SPITE OF THE WIDE range of his work over almost a quarter of a century, Bill Bryson remains best known as a travel writer. Yet, as he told Norman Oder of *Publishers Weekly*, "I stumbled into this genre." *The Lost Continent: Travels in Small-Town America*, documenting a car trip he took around the continental United States in 1987 and 1988 in the wake of his father's death, was not his first book, but it was the first to receive significant attention, at least in his adopted homeland of Britain. His later travel books seemed to confirm both to readers and to critics that this particular genre was Bryson's forte.

In its initial release *The Lost Continent* did not perform as well in the land of Bryson's birth, and Bryson, Oder writes, "acknowledges that *The Lost Continent* lacked balance." He "found a mellower voice in *Notes from a Small Island*," his 1995 book describing his 1994 farewell tour around Britain before returning to America for eight years.

That mixed reception may explain why Bryson's most broadly acclaimed travel book is *A Walk in the Woods:*

Rediscovering America on the Appalachian Trail. Written during the period when Bryson and his family were living in the United States and published a decade after *The Lost Continent*, it exhibits the more tempered sense of humor found in *Notes from a Small Island.* For instance, in both *The Lost Continent* and *A Walk in the Woods*, Bryson visits Gatlinburg, Tennessee, and in both his judgment of the town is negative. In *The Lost Continent*, he makes merciless fun of Americans' obsession with consumerism and kitsch, even while admitting that he shares the obsession. In *A Walk in the Woods*, however, Bryson uses his visit to make a more subtle point about the pace of change in the United States as a whole, which he compares with the relative lack of change on the Appalachian Trail, to the trail's benefit.

Bryson conceived the idea for *A Walk in the Woods* in 1995. "Not long after I moved with my family to a small town in New Hampshire I happened upon a path that vanished into a wood on the edge of town," Bryson writes. Hanover, New Hampshire, the home of Dartmouth College, is one of the entrance points to the Appalachian Trail (or AT, as Bryson abbreviates it throughout the book), "the granddaddy of long hikes." How long is a matter of debate, and Bryson notes that various sources provide different lengths, ranging from a surprisingly definite (though probably not accurate) 2,118.3 miles to 2,200 miles. Stretching from Georgia to Maine, the AT "wanders across fourteen states, through plump, comely hills whose very names—Blue Ridge, Smokies, Cumberlands, Green Mountains, White Mountains—seem an invitation to amble."

Bryson accepts that invitation for a variety of reasons —personal fitness, becoming reacquainted with his native land, the inevitable book—but mostly out of a sense that he should experience the natural beauty and diversity of the AT before that beauty (if not the AT itself) is gone.

One theme that runs through the book is the change —some of it inevitable, much of it not—that the trail and its environs have continued to experience since its formal completion in 1937. While Bryson sounds warnings about climate change and the often destructive effect of government policies on the woodlands of the AT (and, more broadly, the forests of the United States), his message is not one of doom and gloom but of the cycles of nature and of man's interaction with it. There are heartbreaking stories, such as the complete loss of the majestic American chestnut to a blight likely imported from Asia in 1904. In the Appalachians "one tree in every four was a chestnut"; by the time the last chestnut died in 1940, "the Appalachians alone lost four billion trees, a quarter of its cover, in a generation." Such stories of loss are balanced by more encouraging ones, such as the revival of a number of animals that were once close to extinction, including black bears, which Bryson both longs and dreads to see.

For Bryson the choice never comes down to wilderness or people. In the Great Smoky Mountains the Appalachian Trail passes through "treeless, meadowy expanses of mountaintop, up to 250 acres in extent," known as balds. These ecologically diverse areas may have occurred naturally (nobody knows for certain), but as Bryson points out, their survival over the past couple of centuries depended on the activities of farmers, who grazed livestock in these pastures and kept the trees from encroaching. It is a perfect example of the symbiotic relationship between people and their environment. When the National Park Service decided that such grazing interfered with nature, however, the balds began a rather rapid reversion to forest—and, along the way, lost much of the diversity that their former use had encouraged. As Bryson writes, "Within twenty years, there may be no balds left in the Smokies. Ninety plant species have disappeared from the balds since the park was opened in the 1930s. At least twenty-five more are expected to go in the next few years. There is no plan to save them."

In the first half of *A Walk in the Woods*, as he hikes through Georgia, North Carolina, Tennessee, and Virginia, Bryson has mixed feelings about such changes, but by the time he reaches the Delaware Water Gap, between Pennsylvania and New Jersey, he concludes that it would be better in many ways if the guardians of the Appalachian Trail were less concerned about keeping nature pristine. "Personally, I would have been pleased to be walking now through hamlets and past farms rather than through some silent 'protected corridor.'" He contrasts his hike with one that he and his son took through Luxembourg in the early 1990s: "The footpaths we followed spent a lot of time in the woods but also emerged at obliging intervals to take us along sunny back roads and over stiles and through farm fields and hamlets. . . . Each night we slept in an inn and ate in a restaurant with other people. We experienced the whole of

Luxembourg, not just its trees." Nature can be beautiful and terrifying and awe-inspiring, but it gets its meaning from people.

Not surprisingly, therefore, the most engaging parts of the book are those in which Bryson has companions on his walk. When Bryson is hiking a portion of the trail in which he sees few people, *A Walk in the Woods* turns to other subjects, including history and ecology. These subjects are presented in an easygoing and accessible voice, in large part because Bryson's humor continues to shine through. Still, the cast of characters that populates *A Walk in the Woods* and Bryson's interaction with them are as central to the narrative as is the Appalachian Trail itself.

A few days before Bryson set off on his adventure on March 9, 1996, he received a call from a friend he had grown up with in Des Moines. Stephen Katz (the pseudonym Bryson gives him) had appeared in Bryson's 1992 book *Neither Here nor There: Travels in Europe*. The two men had backpacked throughout Europe in the summer of 1973 before Bryson settled in England. (Katz also appears in *The Life and Times of the Thunderbolt Kid*, Bryson's 2006 memoir of growing up in Des Moines in the 1950s.)

Katz volunteered to accompany Bryson on the AT, and Bryson gratefully accepted the offer, unaware that Katz was more out of shape than he. The interaction between the two old friends keeps the narrative moving over long stretches of the trail that would otherwise quickly turn monotonous. Indeed, the reader gets a sense of that monotony when, after a month and a half and 500 miles on the trail, the men take some time off to attend to business and Bryson returns to the trail at the end of May without Katz. The lack of his companion and the constraints of hiking the trail in day-sized chunks (so that he can return to his car each night) leave Bryson dissatisfied. When he and Katz were pushing ever onward, they may have been exhausted and dirty and hungry, but they had a clear goal: to traverse the Appalachian Trail end to end.

When Bryson and Katz had reached Gatlinburg, Tennessee, they saw a wall map of the entire Appalachian Trail, and reality set in. "Of the four feet of trail map before me, reaching approximately from my knees to the top of my head, we had done the bottom two inches," Bryson writes. They decided, "One thing was obvious. We were never going to walk to Maine." Skipping over the rest of the Smoky Mountains, North Carolina, and Tennessee, they picked up the trail again at Roanoke, Virginia. Between there and Front Royal, at the northern end of the Shenandoah Valley, they continued to push forward.

Now, on his day trips without Katz, Bryson could use a lighter pack and sleep in a bed each night, but the sense of accomplishment was lacking. Describing a hike up Mount Moosilauke in the White Mountains of New Hampshire, Bryson writes, "The view from the top was gorgeously panoramic, but it still didn't feel right without Katz, without a full pack. I was home by 4:00 p.m. . . . . You don't hike the Appalachian Trail and then go home and cut the grass."

Throughout the book Bryson returns to this sense of the AT as a singular accomplishment, both in its building and upkeep and in the lives of those who attempt to hike it end to end—especially those who succeed. Their number has increased in recent years, but it is still tiny —a few thousand, compared with the two thirds of the U.S. population who live within a day's drive of the trail. What compels men and women to make the effort, which takes months or, in the case of some who hike the trail in segments, years? Bryson never really finds an answer to that question, despite meeting a number of hikers who have tried. In all, there is a sense of determination, a desire to rise above themselves but also a sense of uncertainty about what awaits them at the end of the trail.

In the end Bryson and Katz share that uncertainty. After spending a few months on his own, Bryson is rejoined by Katz to hike the final section of the Appalachian Trail—a forbidding stretch of forest known as the Hundred Mile Wilderness, "99.7 miles of boreal forest trail without a store, house, telephone, or paved road." Commenting on this last portion of the trail, which ends at Mount Katahdin, the northernmost point, Bryson writes, "It is the remotest section of the entire AT. If something goes wrong in the Hundred Mile Wilderness, you are on your own. You could die of an infected blood blister out there."

For both men, hiking once again with a full pack is tough. Unable to keep up with Bryson, Katz solves the problem by discarding many of the heavier items in his pack —including food they will need in the wilderness. Luckily, they had started thirty-eight miles outside of the Hundred Mile Wilderness, so they had one more chance to stock up before beginning the last stretch of the trail, which most hikers finish in seven to ten days.

On their second day in the wilderness, Bryson and Katz get separated and spend the night apart, neither knowing whether the other is still alive. The writing is on the wall. "We decided to leave the endless trail and stop pretending we were mountain men because we weren't," Bryson admits. Finding a dirt logging road, they hitch a ride to Milo, Maine, and officially end their trek.

What had it all meant? "I had come to realize," Bryson writes, "that I didn't have any feelings towards the AT that weren't confused and contradictory. I was weary of the trail, but still strangely in its thrall; found the endless slog tedious but irresistible; grew tired of the boundless woods but admired their boundlessness; enjoyed the escape from civilization and ached for its comforts. I wanted to quit and to do this forever, sleep in a bed and in a tent, see what was over the next hill and never see a hill again."

In the final pages of *A Walk in the Woods,* Bryson decides that those contradictions may well have been the point. Hiking the Appalachian Trail, Bryson suggests, is less about covering every last inch of it by foot than about the journey and what hikers encounter and learn on the way. A sentence on the final page sums it all up in three short words: "I came home." Yet when he and Katz came home, they were different men from the men who started the hike six months earlier.

Critical reaction to *A Walk in the Woods* was almost universally positive. *Booklist* declared, "Bryson's book is a marvelous description and history of the trail and the mountains," and his "great good humor makes this a journey worth taking." *Library Journal* described the book as "amiable" and added, "Bryson shares some truly laugh-out-loud moments, as well as some reflective commentary, on the state of people, politics, and life along the trail." In a separate review, *Library Journal* noted that the book "is a blend of personal experience and social commentary that tackles issues large and small, from the author's fear of bears to the failure of the U.S. government to sufficiently preserve natural habitats." *Publishers Weekly*, after proclaiming that Bryson "records the misadventure with insight and elegance," declared, "He is a popular author in Britain and his impeccably graceful and witty style deserves a large American audience as well." Indeed, *A Walk in the Woods* was Bryson's breakout book in the United States. It enjoyed as much popularity in Britain, where the *New Statesman* admired Bryson's ability to write "casually and comfortably" and raved that, "His graphic description of his likely reaction to encountering bears in the woods may be the funniest bit of scatological humour in the whole of modern travel literature."

The Mother Tongue

Despite his reputation as a travel writer, Bill Bryson's first published book was a small volume entitled *The Book of Blunders* (1982), a collection of amusing and embarrassing true stories—often no longer than a sentence or two and in no case more than five or six—from around the world. The book might have been lost to the ages, except that, after

Bryson's other works garnered critical acclaim and significant sales, Warner Books released a new edition entitled *Bizarre World* (1995), which went through multiple printings.

Bryson's first major published work was *The Penguin Dictionary of Troublesome Words*. As Bryson notes in the introduction to a later edition, "When I put together *The Penguin Dictionary of Troublesome Words* (as it then was) in 1983, I was a young copy editor on the London *Times*, and it was a fundamental part of my job to be sensitive to and particular about points of usage. It was why they employed me, after all, and I took the responsibility seriously."

Not all editors are good writers, and many accomplished writers would make poor editors; over the course of his career Bryson has successfully combined both abilities. That *Bryson's Dictionary of Troublesome Words* (as the current edition is known) is a useful style guide for editors is not surprising; after all, he writes, "Nearly everything in it arose as the product of questions encountered during the course of daily newspaper work." It is also a useful volume for writers, and, in fact, Bryson's often humorous entries in the dictionary read more like instructions to the writer than to the editor. Moreover, the wry wit and the variety of examples of errors drawn from major British and American publications make the book attractive even to the average reader who simply delights in the intricacies of the English language.

Bryson's Dictionary of Troublesome Words displays early indications of Bryson's fascination with the English language, which would reach full flower in his 1990 book *The Mother Tongue: English and How It Got That Way*. Billed as a history of the English language, *The Mother Tongue* packs into fewer than 250 pages a remarkable amount of information not only on English but on the development of language in general and the differences, both subtle and stark, that exist among the many languages of the world.

In the hands of a professional linguist, such material might be interesting but dry (or perhaps only dry). Bryson, however, presents the subject matter as he approached it himself: as a writer and a reader who may find the eccentricities of the English language at times frustrating but who always loves the richness of the language and its literature. He returns time and again in the book to the idea that English is the most expressive of all modern languages, to the point that one begins to suspect that this variety, as much as the accidents of history and the political and economic might of the Anglo-American world, has something to do with the rise of English as a global language. Still, as Bryson himself cautions, in chapter 12 ("English as a World Language"), "Most people speak [English] not because it gives them pleasure to help out American and British monoglots who cannot be troubled to learn a few words of their language, . . . but because they need it to function in the world at large."

Bryson begins *The Mother Tongue* with a sentence that sets the humorous tone for the book: "More than 300 million people in the world speak English and the rest, it sometimes seems, try to." Later on, in chapter 12, he notes that this 300 or 350 million is an estimate of native speakers. More important perhaps, "No other language . . . is spoken as an official language in more countries—forty-four, as against twenty-seven for French and twenty for Spanish—and none is spoken over a wider area of the globe." Of course, those who speak English do so in a variety of ways and at differing levels of proficiency; the mere fact that two people speak it is no guarantee that they will be able to understand each other completely or even well enough to avoid embarrassing misunderstandings.

Such misunderstandings most obviously arise when one of the speakers is not a native speaker, and Bryson provides a number of examples, such as these instructions to English-speaking drivers in Japan: "When a passenger of the foot heave in sight, tootle the horn. Trumpet at him melodiously at first, but if he still obstacles your passage, then tootle him with vigor." Even between two competent native speakers, geographical differences in usage may lead to embarrassing moments. In Britain, Bryson writes in chapter 11 ("Old World, New World"), *"to be stuffed* is distinctly rude, so that if you say at a dinner party, 'I couldn't eat another thing; I'm stuffed,' an embarrassing silence will fall over the table. (You may recognize the voice of experience in this.)"

Such linguistic diversity, Bryson notes, helps explain both the richness of English and the sometimes frustrating inability to establish reasonably complete rules of spelling, pronunciation, and grammar. In chapter after chapter, Bryson highlights the inconsistencies of the language and does his best to explain how they have arisen. Many, he notes, come from the fact that English, perhaps more than any other language, has a long history of borrowing words, spelling, and even grammar from other languages. "We take words from almost anywhere—*shampoo* from India, *chaparral* from the Basques, *caucus* from the Algonquin Indians, *ketchup* from China, *potato* from Haiti, *sofa* from Arabia, *boondocks* from the Tagalog language of the Philippines, *slogan* from Gaelic."

Indeed, though its roots are in Old English, a Germanic language, modern English has been heavily shaped by centuries of conflict and conquest, especially by the Scandinavians and the Norman French. Thus, Bryson notes in chapter 4 ("The First Thousand Years") that "animals in the field usually were called by English names (sheep, cow, ox), but once cooked and brought to the table, they were generally given French names (beef, mutton, veal, bacon)." The Norman conquest of England in 1066 brought with it not only a wide variety of new words but changes in pronunciation; some Anglo-Saxon words took on French sounds, and vice versa.

Also, until as late as the mid-nineteenth century, English spelling tended to be much more fluid, and changes in pronunciation were often reflected in new spellings. Occasionally, Bryson notes, the opposite occurred: As spellings changed, additional letters added to words sometimes worked their way into the popular pronunciation, which itself eventually became standard. Thus, "*descrive* (or *descryve*) became *describe*, *perfet* (or *parfet*) became *perfect*, *verdit* became *verdict*, and *aventure* had a *d* hammered into its first syllable. At first all these inserted letters were as silent as the *b* in *debt*, but eventually they became voiced."

Still, despite the confusion that the joyous jumble of spelling and pronunciation can produce in English speakers and readers (not to mention those attempting to learn the language), changes in spelling have generally arisen organically, over long periods of time. In chapter 8, "Spelling," Bryson notes that, "by late in the [19th] century it seemed as if every eminent person on both sides of the Atlantic—including [Charles] Darwin, [Alfred] Tennyson, Arthur Conan Doyle, James A. H. Murray (the first editor of the *Oxford English Dictionary*), and of course [Mark] Twain —was pushing for spelling reform. It is hard to say which is the more remarkable, the number of influential people who became interested in spelling reform or the little effect they had on it."

There may be a reason that spelling reform has never caught on, and Bryson alludes to it at the end of his chapter on spelling. "What simplified spelling systems gain in terms of consistency they often throw away in terms of clarity. *Eight* may be a peculiar way of spelling the number that follows seven, but it certainly helps to distinguish it from the past tense of *eat*." Thus, memorizing irregular spellings may be the lesser of two evils—and, considering that such spellings can often provide clues to the meaning and origin of a word, it is perhaps overstating the case to consider irregular spelling an evil at all. After enumerating several other such examples where clarity might be lost, Bryson makes his argument unanswerable with his customary wit: "Perplexity and ambiguity would reign (or rain or rein)."

For other languages, such problems are solved (or at least addressed) by organizations that set standards—the most well known being the Académie Française, which was established almost four centuries ago to bring order to the French language. English has never had such a standards-producing body; perhaps the closest that it has ever come to one is the *Oxford English Dictionary* (*OED*), compiled (in its initial edition) over a span of almost fifty years, from 1879 through 1928. As Bryson points out, the sheer size of the *OED* indicates the scope of the problem. The second edition, published in 1989, has "615,000 entries, 2,412,000 supporting quotations, almost 60 million words of exposition, and about 350 million keystrokes of text." (The new edition of the *OED*, still (in 2009) several years away from publication, is expected to contain more than one million entries.)

Even among the publishers of dictionaries, Bryson notes, there is no consensus about whether such volumes should be descriptive (listing all current usages and meanings for words, without prejudice) or prescriptive (preferring established usages and meanings over newer ones). Most are a mix: The *OED*, largely descriptive, provides the history of usage for each word, but such a history in itself performs something of a prescriptive function, as it gives greater weight to older usages (or at least established ones).

On this question Bryson himself is divided. The writer and lover of wordplay declares, "One of the undoubted virtues of English is that it is a fluid and democratic language in which meanings shift and change in response to the pressures of common usage rather than the dictates of committees. . . . To interfere with that process is arguably both arrogant and futile . . ." Yet the editor in Bryson sees that "there is a case for resisting change" (and a volume such as *Bryson's Dictionary of Troublesome Words* would make no sense otherwise). Bryson concludes, "As John Ciardi observed, resistance may in the end prove futile, but at least it tests the changes and makes them prove their worth."

Indeed, over the years, many such changes have been found worthy. English speakers go through periodic bursts of creativity, such as the period from 1500 to 1650; of that century and a half Bryson writes, "Between 10,000 and 12,000 words were coined, of which about half still exist." Shakespeare himself "used 17,677 words in his writings, of which at least one tenth had never been used before." For every word that proves its worth, there is at least one that does not. As Bryson notes, "Shakespeare gave us the useful *gloomy*, but failed with *barky* and *brisky* (formed after the same pattern but somehow never catching on) and failed equally with *conflux*, *vastidity*, and *tortive*."

English in America, as Bryson demonstrates in chapter 11 ("Old World, New World"), has adopted many words from a variety of sources. Variants of thousands of American Indian words, of course, are in common use today as place names in the United States, though, as Bryson notes, "we borrowed no more than three or four dozen Indian words for everyday objects—among them *canoe*, *raccoon*, *hammock*, and *tobacco*." Other Indian words entered the language by way of borrowings from the early Spanish and French settlers, from whom American English also borrowed many native terms.

Such borrowings, however, are only part of the reason why some English speakers on both sides of the Atlantic, even until well into the twentieth century, had come to believe that American English and British English were evolving into separate languages. Indeed, as late as 1978, "in a speech to 800 librarians in Chicago, Robert Burchfield, then the chief editor of the *Supplement to the Oxford English Dictionary*, noted his belief that British English and American English were moving apart so inexorably that within 200 years they could be mutually unintelligible." One of Bryson's own books, *Bill Bryson's African Diary*, provides an interesting example. In it Bryson uses a number of British spellings, expressions, and names for items—none of which makes the book unintelligible to the American reader but certainly may cause such a reader to stumble momentarily. (There is a certain irony in the fact that Bryson wrote *African Diary* in 2002, while living in New Hampshire.) In another of Bryson's books, *Notes from a Small Island*, there are significant differences between the British and American editions, most of which were clearly made to eliminate the need to explain British terms (such as *crisps*, for potato chips) to an American audience.

Over the years many British speakers have frowned on the freedom with which Americans combine existing English words to create new ones—or simply make up new expressions, often referred to as Americanisms. "The quintessential Americanism," Bryson writes, "without any doubt was *O.K.*" He argues that *O.K.* (or *OK,* as it is now usually spelled) is "the most grammatically versatile of words"; it can, in various circumstances, be used as almost any part of speech. Bryson examines the controversy over the origins of *OK* and presents a plausible theory (put forth by Allen

Walker Read of Columbia University) that it emerged as sort of an early nineteenth-century version of text messaging —as one of several "abbreviations based on intentional illiteracies" (in this case, for "oll korrect"). Whether Read's theory is OK is debatable; what is not is that *OK* is "arguably America's single greatest gift to international discourse."

In his final chapter, "The Future of English," Bryson notes that the language remains in flux. In the United States an increasing number of new immigrants speak a language other than English (mostly Spanish) as their primary language. Yet the greatest threat to English might well come from native speakers, whose mastery of the language declined over the second half of the twentieth century (especially in America). In that light, concerns about differences of dialect and usage seem trivial. English is not likely to splinter into separate languages, the way that the Romance languages evolved from Latin, if only because, as Bryson notes, "movies, television, books, magazines, record albums, business contacts, tourism—all these are powerfully binding influences." Today, the Internet, which was in its infancy at the time Bryson wrote *The Mother Tongue,* might also be included.

The real danger of such "binding influences" is that they will have an homogenizing effect. Bryson, the writer and lover of language, voiced this concern: "If we should be worrying about anything to do with the future of English, it should be not that the various strands will drift apart but that they will grow indistinguishable. And what a sad, sad loss that would be."

While Bill Bryson's guides to English usage (*Bryson's Dictionary of Troublesome Words* and *Bryson's Dictionary for Writers and Editors*) have generally received positive reviews, his writings on the history of the English language have received more mixed ones. *The Writer* refers to Bryson as "a language maven" and *The Mother Tongue* and *Made in America* as "lighthearted and informative books." *Publishers Weekly* wrote that Bryson's "blend of linguistic anecdote and Anglo-Saxon cultural history . . . keeps us turning pages" yet declared, "Depth of treatment is not, however, to be found here" and summed up its review in its headline: "Linguistics as pop science." The *New York Times* notes that, although Bryson believes that "English can survive anything," he "leaves the reader in a minor quandary. What if English evolved to the point that every country had its version?" In that case, the review concludes, "the only consolation would be that there would still be room for amusing books like Mr. Bryson's."

A Short History of Nearly Everything

To many readers and critics, Bill Bryson's 2003 book *A Short History of Nearly Everything* seemed a departure from his previous works. It is, after all, neither a travel book nor a book about language. Moreover, other than whatever knowledge of nature and biology might help him stay alive as he braved the wilder stretches of the Appalachian Trail or the more desolate portions of the Australian Outback, Bryson had shown no particular interest in science in his previous

A sudden realization that he knew very little about science in general, and life on this planet in particular, led Bill Bryson to write *A Short History of Nearly Everything.*

books. Indeed, in the introduction to *A Short History*, he admits as much and attributes his lack of interest to a 1950s era textbook whose deadening prose quickly dampened the fires of excitement that the book's illustrations had initially ignited. "There seemed to be," Bryson writes, "a mystifying universal conspiracy among textbook authors to make certain the material they dealt with never strayed too near the realm of the mildly interesting and was always at least a long-distance phone call from the frankly interesting."

All of that changed for Bryson in the late 1990s as he stared out the window of a jet on a transpacific flight. "It occurred to me with a certain uncomfortable forcefulness," he writes, "that I didn't know the first thing about the only planet I was ever going to live on." Beginning with "why the oceans were salty but the Great Lakes weren't," his thoughts ranged over the extent of the gaps in his knowledge, until "I became gripped by a quiet, unwonted urge to know a little about these matters and to understand how people figured them out."

How scientists work things out is at the heart of *A Short History of Nearly Everything*, and it is what makes this book (despite its wide-ranging subject matter) fit comfortably into the body of Bryson's work. *A Short History* begins at the big bang—"about 12 billion to 13.5 billion years" ago— and concludes in the 1990s. The almost 500 pages of text and 38 pages of notes present the current state of scientific knowledge largely through a series of historical narratives that explain how scientists arrived at the current understanding of the universe. Along the way, readers are exposed to the sciences of astronomy, geology, biology, chemistry, physics, and paleontology (among others) in a manner that is likely to make them want to explore at least some of these fields in greater depth.

A Short History is, in other words, the very opposite of the dry textbook that blunted Bryson's own curiosity as a young student. Rather than a collection of facts to be memorized, the book contains a multitude of "facts" that no one would want to memorize, because some of them are now known to be mistaken. As each narrative unfolds, readers learn the current scientific consensus on the age of the Earth, or the structure of atoms, or what caused the extinction of the dinosaurs, or how man may have evolved into modern *Homo sapiens*, but the book is even more about how scientists came to understand these things than about what scientists now think the right answers are (though it is about that, too).

For that reason Bryson's narrative style, developed in his travel books, serves him as well here as it does in his books on the evolution of the English language (*The Mother Tongue* and *Made in America*) and his more recent biography *Shakespeare: The World as Stage* (2007). Bryson set out with the idea "to see if it isn't possible to understand and appreciate —marvel at, enjoy even—the wonder and accomplishments of science at a level that isn't too technical or demanding, but isn't entirely superficial either."

Bryson reaches this goal by breaking the history of science into a series of narratives. Learning how people came to understand that space is mostly empty rather than filled (as scientists believed for hundreds of years) with an undetectable substance called ether is much more interesting than simply knowing that, in deep space, atoms live quite solitary lives (as Bryson notes, that is one of the reasons why space is so cold, since heat is transmitted by the contact between atoms).

Thanks to Bryson's technique, readers do not need to sit down and read *A Short History of Nearly Everything* from cover to cover but can choose those sections and chapters that most interest them. Because of the way Bryson ties many of the narratives together, however, those who read the entire book will emerge with a more complete understanding of how all the sciences relate.

One thing that quickly becomes obvious is just how recent much of the knowledge of the physical world really is. To most readers, the term "modern science" refers to the development of chemistry and physics in the seventeenth and eighteenth centuries and modern astronomy in the two centuries before that. However, geology, Bryson points out, did not become much of a discipline until the nineteenth century, and then it was primarily the work of amateurs.

Scientific understanding of each of these fields, however, has changed dramatically in just the past century. The theory that space was filled with ether, for instance, was still believed by one notable British physicist as late as 1909. Most textbooks today describe the sudden extinction of the dinosaurs 65 million years ago as a result of a meteor crashing into Earth, but that idea did not arise until the late 1970s. Before that, scientists assumed that the extinction had happened gradually, over the course of millions of years.

"As late as 1988," Bryson comments, "more than half of all American paleontologists contacted in a survey continued to believe that the extinction of the dinosaurs was in no way related to an asteroid or cometary impact."

Continental drift; plate tectonics (the theory that the earth's crust, moving in plates, throws up mountains); ice ages; evolution; the fundamental role that DNA plays in human life—all of these either were discovered in the twentieth century or first gained widespread acceptance then. Aspects of each, Bryson stresses, are still in dispute. Every time scientists think that they have come close to knowing all that there is to know about a particular branch of science, something comes along to indicate that they have really only begun to scratch the surface.

Ordinary science textbooks may make note of previous theories, but they rarely attempt to explain why scientists might have held them. Bryson, however, recognizes that there are lessons to be learned even from those who got things wrong—not the least of which, perhaps, is that current theories may not explain everything and may themselves give way someday under the weight of newfound evidence.

The popular conception of science is that it is much like mathematics—in mathematics there is always one right, exact answer to be found. Yet Newtonian physics, far from being supplanted by the theories of Albert Einstein, remains valid in most of the circumstances of everyday life. While Einstein's general theory of relativity relies on a "cosmological constant, which arbitrarily counterbalanced the effects of gravity" in order to make it work, it still accurately describes what is known of the relationship between time and space. While Einstein called the cosmological constant the biggest blunder of his life, Bryson notes, "It now appears that he may have gotten things right after all."

Since textbooks are designed to teach facts, they must necessarily take a snapshot of scientific knowledge at a particular time and present it as a system. They may do so with caveats and stress that hypotheses need to be tested and that theories may be only approximations of reality, but it is hard for them not to give the impression that physics or chemistry or biology or astronomy consists essentially of what scientists know *right now*.

Bryson takes a different approach, one that is reflected in the book's very title. Just as no country or institution can be fully understood apart from its history, so, too, science's history is integral to science itself. In a sense, knowing *why* I know something is almost more important than *that* I know it. Knowing why helps me to understand and interpret new knowledge when I discover it.

Bryson's book is full of examples of serendipity; a scientist searching for the answer to one question uncovers something completely unexpected. For instance, it is now known that Yellowstone National "Park is a supervolcano, an area of 2.2 million acres in which the earth's crust barely covers a huge pool of magma—"molten rock that rises from at least 125 miles down in the Earth." In the 1960s, Bob Christiansen of the U.S. Geological Survey had attempted to pinpoint Yellowstone's volcanic activity, but he never would have succeeded if NASA had not "decided to test some new high-altitude cameras by taking photographs of Yellowstone, copies of which some thoughtful official passed on to the park authorities on the assumption that they might make a nice blow-up for one of the visitors' centers."

Dinosaurs have been discovered by literally tripping over their bones; the greatest lode of fossils ever found was, according to legend, discovered when a horse twisted its ankle. Bryson indicates that this last story is apocryphal, but even so, it nicely illustrates how much of the knowledge of Earth has been gained almost by accident.

Simply discovering something does not ensure that scientists will understand what has been discovered. Bryson uncovers several stories of scientists who made important discoveries—the first dinosaur bone, for instance—who do not receive credit for their finds because they thought they were looking at something else or at something unimportant.

Bryson has divided *A Short History* into six parts, providing a natural progression both through the sciences and through history. Part 1, "Lost in the Cosmos," takes the reader from the big bang through the creation of the solar system to the formation of Earth and the Moon. Part 2, "The Size of the Earth," introduces geology and the physical sciences. Part 3, "A New Age Dawns," gives a glimpse of the world that cannot be seen with the naked eye—the world of atoms and subatomic forces and particle physics.

In part 4, "Dangerous Planet," Bryson picks up a theme that recurs throughout the rest of the book—that life on Earth is somewhat precarious. Between comets that occasionally crash into the planet and eruptions from below, there are tremendous forces that threaten all living creatures on the planet, forces about which essentially nothing can be done. Yet life, as Bryson points out in part 5, "Life Itself," has been remarkably resilient ever since it appeared on Earth approximately 3.85 billion years ago, "stunningly early," Bryson notes, since "Earth's surface didn't become *solid* until about 3.9 billion years ago." Life is not only resilient but abundant and found in virtually every place man has ever looked—including at temperatures (both high and low) and at atmospheric pressures that should make it impossible for life to exist.

While Bryson expertly navigates his way through a number of scientific controversies throughout the book, it is only in the final chapters of part 5 and in part 6, "The Road to Us," that Bryson gets heavily into material that has been the focus of public debate in recent years, especially in the United States. His discussion of Darwinian evolution is dispassionate and benefits from Bryson's ability to put the development of the theory in historical context. Darwin was not the first advocate of evolution, and indeed, when he first presented his particular theory publicly, "a Professor Haughton of Dublin," Bryson notes, declared "that all that was new in them was false, and what was true was old."

In light of current controversies over evolution, it is interesting to learn that "Darwin never ceased being tormented by his ideas. He referred to himself as 'the Devil's Chaplain' and said that revealing the theory felt 'like confessing a murder.'" Bryson also notes that, in 1802 (fifty-six

As Bryson notes in *A Short History*, Darwin's theory of evolution remained controversial, even to Darwin himself.

years before Darwin announced his theory publicly and almost three decades before Darwin took his celebrated trip on HMS *Beagle*), the English theologian William Paley first put forth the "argument from design." The complexity of nature, Paley believed, "was proof of its design" by an outside intelligence. Even Darwin admitted that it was hard to explain how certain organs could evolve as a result of natural selection. As Bryson notes in the book, Darwin, in a letter to a friend, declared, "The eye to this day gives me a cold shudder."

Bryson does not directly enter the current political fray over evolution nor over global warming, which he mentions in his section on ice ages in part 6. What he does make clear, in the final chapter, is that no other single species that has ever existed has had as much ability "to look after life in our lonely cosmos" and to affect the future of Earth as the human species has. "But here's an extremely salient point: we have been chosen, by fate or Providence or whatever you wish to call it. As far as we can tell, we are the best there is. We may be all there is."

Throughout *A Short History of Nearly Everything*, Bryson emphasizes how remarkable all human life is, considering all of the events that had to fall into just the right order (and, just as important, all of the things that could have happened but did not) to result in the particular combination of genes that makes each person unique. That "luck," as he calls it, carries with it a great responsibility. As humans, "We enjoy not only the privilege of existence but also the singular ability to appreciate it and even, in a multitude of ways, to make it better. It is a talent," he concludes, "we have only barely begun to grasp."

The list of awards won by *A Short History of Nearly Everything* (including the 2005 Descartes Prize for Science Communication and the 2004 Aventis Prize) reflects the critical acclaim that the book has garnered since its publication. *Book* calls it "a mind-bending odyssey through the annals of scientific theory," while noting that Bryson "could well face charges of oversimplification"; yet, among authors of science texts for a popular audience, "few have proven more lucid than he." The *Spectator* admits that "there are people much better qualified than Bill Bryson to attempt a project of this magnitude," yet "none of them ... can write fluent Brysonese, which, as pretty much the entire Western reading public now knows, is an appealing mixture of self-deprecation, wryness and punnery." In the end, however, the *Spectator* concludes that "the book doesn't quite come off," partly because of the subject matter itself ("much of what Bryson is describing is, well, indescribable") and partly because "the sublime subject matter doesn't allow Bryson to do his standard self-deprecating shtick." *Kirkus Reviews* declared that Bryson is "a man who knows how to track down an explanation and make it confess" and that he "renders clear the evolution of continental drift, atomic structure, singularity, the extinction of the dinosaur, and a mighty host of other subjects in self-contained chapters that can be taken at a bite, rather than read wholesale." The book, *Kirkus Reviews* concludes, contains "loads of good explaining, with reminders, time and again, of how much remains unknown, neatly putting the depth of science into perspective." *Publishers Weekly* found the book "great for Bryson fans" but noted that "readers in the field will already have studied this information more in-depth in the originals and may find themselves questioning the point of a breakneck tour of the sciences that contributes nothing novel." *Library Journal*, on the other hand, declared in a starred review, "Although Bryson clearly intends this book for general readers, subject specialists will also enjoy his wry takes."

The Life and Times of the Thunderbolt Kid

While most reviewers continue to describe Bryson as a travel writer, his published works have always contained an element of memoir. His first commercial success, *The Lost Continent*, was billed as a travel book, but Bryson often offers only the most basic description of the towns and cities he visits during his nearly 14,000-mile trip across the United States. *The Lost Continent* is perhaps as much a memoir of his father (whose death occasioned Bryson's trip), of life in the 1950s and early 1960s, and of the vanishing American "car culture," as it is a travel book.

Other works, especially the newspaper columns collected in *I'm a Stranger Here Myself*, have the feel of a memoir as well, though on a limited scale. *I'm a Stranger Here Myself* provides a slice of the life of the Bryson family in the years after they moved to the United States in 1995, as well as a partial glimpse of the life of the country during that same time.

TALKN' ABOUT: BILL BRYSON

HE GREW UP IN DES MOINES, IOWA, BUT IS CONSIDERED AN AMERICAN-BORN BRITISH WRITER, BECAUSE HE'S LIVED MOST OF HIS ADULT LIFE IN ENGLAND. THAT'S WHY, ALSO, YOU HEAR A BRITISH LILT IN HIS VOICE IF YOU'VE EVER LISTENED TO HIS FUNNY AND GIFTED READINGS OF HIS FUNNY AND SMART BOOKS ABOUT TRAVEL AND SCIENCE AND WELL, EVERYTHING. HE MET HIS WIFE CYNTHIA, WHILE WORKING AT A PSYCHIATRIC HOSPITAL IN SURREY, ENGLAND. THEY HAVE 4 KIDS, AND ACCORDING TO HIS WRITING, SHE DOES ALL THE COOKING. BRYSON EVENTUALLY WOULD BECOME A JOURNALIST, WORKING FOR THE TIMES AND THE INDEPENDENT. HE LEFT JOURNALISM IN 1987 AND BEGAN WRITING HIS BOOKS, WHICH INCLUDE THE LOST CONTINENT (MY FRIEND, MATT'S FAVORITE), NIETHER HERE NOR THERE: TRAVELS IN EUROPE A WALK IN THE WOODS (MY STEPMOM, PAM'S, FAVORITE), & IN A SUNBURNED COUNTRY (WHICH A LADY AT MY WORK WAS READING FOR HER TRIP TO AUSTRALIA). HIS MOST RECENT BOOK IS A MEMOIR CALLED THE ADVENTURES OF THE THUNDERBOLT KID. DUE OUT IN OCTOBER!

In *The Life and Times of the Thunderbolt Kid*, Bryson embraced the memoir genre, but his view was happy and nostalgic, unlike so many other looks back.

With his 2006 work, *The Life and Times of the Thunder-bolt Kid: A Memoir,* however, Bryson fully embraced the genre, as the subtitle acknowledges. While not a strict chronological retelling of Bryson's early life, the book offers a richly textured narrative of life in a midwestern city in the 1950s and early 1960s, with occasional glances forward to the end of that decade and Bryson's graduation from high school.

"I can't imagine there has ever been a more gratifying time or place to be alive than America in the 1950s," Bryson writes in "Hometown," chapter 1 of *Thunderbolt Kid.* This sentiment led some reviewers—even those who praised the memoir—to characterize the book as more nostalgia than history. Yet Bryson's nostalgia is itself a part of the history of the era, which, for most Americans, was marked by a level of optimism not seen before or since, as Bryson himself notes.

In an interview with Emma Brockes in the *Guardian,* Bryson captures some of that feeling: "There was a real excitement there, that we've just lost, about future possibilities. If you were a kid you really did expect, any day, that we'd all have jet-packs or be going on vacation to Mars, and magazines were constantly full of articles with wonderful artists' impressions of what the world would be like any time now. And that's completely gone. Nobody gets excited about the future at all, ever. The future is something we find depressing and worrisome."

The 1950s had their own set of worries, even in Des Moines, where Bryson was born and where almost all of *Thunderbolt Kid* takes place. Chapter 11, entitled "What,

Me Worry?" (the famous tagline of *MAD Magazine*, itself a product of the 1950s), opens with a reproduction of a *Collier's* magazine cover. The cover bears the title "HIROSHIMA, U.S.A.: Can Anything Be Done About It?" and features a photorealistic painting of a nuclear mushroom cloud rising over Manhattan.

The possibility of nuclear war occupied the minds of many Americans in the 1950s and early 1960s, and in both chapter 11 and chapter 7 ("Boom!"), Bryson discusses the preparations made to survive a nuclear war. Schoolchildren practiced crouching under their desks with their hands over their heads (a maneuver known as the "duck and cover"), while construction companies built both public and private fallout shelters and even concrete-reinforced homes that would supposedly withstand a nuclear attack.

As Bryson points out, the 1950s were marked by "a curious blend of undiluted optimism and a kind of eager despair." More than 20 percent of Americans in 1955 thought that mankind would disappear from the earth by 1960, "Yet the very people who claimed to expect death at any moment were at the same time busily buying new homes, digging swimming pools, investing in stocks and bonds and pension plans, and generally behaving like people who expect to live a long time."

Bryson ends chapter 11 with the revelation, culled from the archives of the defunct Soviet Union in 1991, that the world came much closer to the brink of full-scale nuclear war during the Cuban Missile Crisis of October 1962 than anyone had imagined. "The Soviets in fact already had about

Collier's

15c

August 5, 1950

HIROSHIMA, U.S.A.

Can Anything Be Done About It?

In the 1950s and early 1960s, the threat of atomic war seemed imminent. The fear that the Soviet Union would do to us what we had done to Japan at the end of World War II is captured famously in this *Collier's* magazine cover.

170 nuclear missiles positioned on Cuban soil . . . Imagine an America with 170 of its largest cities—which, just for the record, would include Des Moines—wiped out. And of course it wouldn't have stopped there."

For Bryson and his friends, however, these concerns were less important than the trials and tribulations of growing up. Television was just coming into its heyday, and Bryson pays due notice to the changes that the medium effected in American society over the coming decades, as people spent more time in front of their television sets and less time with family and neighbors. Even clothing, furniture, and food were influenced by television, with TV dinners being served on TV trays to family members dressed in special sportswear designed not for play but for TV watching.

Color television arrived in Bryson's neighborhood near the end of the decade, but few people could afford it. Bryson recalls "when Mr. Kiessler on St. John's Road bought an enormous RCA Victor Consolette" two years before anyone else in the neighborhood had color television. "On Saturday evenings the children of the neighborhood would steal into his yard and stand in his flower beds to watch a program called *My Living Doll* through the double window behind his sofa."

Even with the dawn of the age of television, Bryson and his friends, like most children in the 1950s, spent far more time outside than children do today. There is a carefree sense of freedom that runs through *Thunderbolt Kid*. Bryson frequently traveled a couple of miles from his neighborhood into downtown Des Moines, population 200,000, on the bus or, more often, on foot and without an adult. Both of his parents worked at the *Des Moines Register* and the *Tribune* (the morning and evening editions of the local newspaper, respectively), and Bryson attended schools in his neighborhood, so he was often unsupervised. "By second grade," he writes, "I was pretty routinely declining my mother's daily entreaties to rise," and so he was frequently absent from school because his mother, exasperated, would simply leave him at home.

With his father, a sportswriter, often traveling on weekends, Bryson would make the trek downtown most Fridays to meet his mother after work for dinner at Bishop's Buffet (a famous midwestern restaurant chain) and a movie. He describes his routine—entering downtown Des Moines from the west, through a neighborhood with "a slight but agreeably seedy air," before moving into the business district. He always visited the same stores: Pinky's, a joke and novelty store; Frankel's, a men's clothing store whose mezzanine level was a popular place (for boys, especially) from which to observe the crowds below; and Younkers, one of the most famous department stores in the midwest, which employed 1,200 people and attracted shoppers from miles around with a combination of service and elegance. "Generally," Bryson writes, "I would call in at the long soda fountain at Woolworth's for one of their celebrated Green Rivers, a refreshing concoction of syrupy green fizz that was the schoolboy aperitif of the 1950s." These places exist now only in memory; they have fallen victim to the "progress" so admired by Americans in the 1950s. (Green

Rivers, however, are still being served in small local ice-cream parlors in the midwest.)

Much of that progress centered on labor-saving gadgets and the automobile. "By the closing years of the 1950s," Bryson writes in chapter 13 ("The Pubic Years"), "most people—certainly most middle-class people—had pretty much everything they had ever dreamed of, so increasingly there was nothing much to do with their wealth but buy more and bigger versions of things they didn't truly require: second cars, lawn tractors, double-width fridges, hi-fis with bigger speakers and more knobs to twiddle, extra phones and televisions, room intercoms, gas grills, kitchen gadgets, snowblowers, you name it." Bryson is ambivalent about the changes: On the one hand, he, like most children in the 1950s, was enamored of technology; on the other, looking back fifty years later, he recognizes that the sense of joy and wonder and optimism contained the seeds of its own destruction.

"According to the Gallup Organization 1957 was the happiest year ever recorded in the United States of America," Bryson notes. In chapter 5, "The Pursuit of Pleasure," he argues that "fun was a different kind of thing in the 1950s, mostly because there wasn't so much of it. That is not, let me say, a bad thing. . . . You learned to wait for your pleasures, and to appreciate them when they came." As all the gadgets and entertainment and labor-saving devices became ubiquitous, "what had once been utterly delightful was now becoming very slightly, rather strangely unfulfilling. People were beginning to discover that joyous consumerism is a world of diminishing returns."

Americans began to work harder, but they were spending more of their hard-earned money. Other changes were in the wind. In the mid–1950s, "America had thirty-two million children aged twelve or under," but after 1957 the birthrate began to drop for the first time since the end of World War II. The 1960s would be a decade of teenagers, but the 1950s were "Kid World," the heyday of young children with healthy imaginations, like Bryson himself, who created the persona of the Thunderbolt Kid, "the modest superhero of the prairies," after discovering "hanging behind the furnace . . . a woolen jersey of rare fineness." The deep green jersey featured a golden satin thunderbolt.

"It was, obviously," writes Bryson, "the Sacred Jersey of Zap, left to me by King Volton, my late natural father, who had brought me to Earth in a silver spaceship." Combined with the accoutrements of television and comic-book heroes, the jersey formed the uniform of a superhero endowed with "ThunderVision™," which could be used "to strip away undergarments without damaging skin or outer clothing" and as "a powerful weapon to vaporize irritating people."

Despite his prominent place in the title, the Thunderbolt Kid makes relatively few appearances in the memoir, serving more as a framing device than as an essential part of the narrative. Eventually, in one of the most poignant passages in the book, the Thunderbolt Kid's back story changes, as Bryson gains a newfound respect for his father.

After *Thunderbolt Kid* was released, Bryson told an interviewer for the *Guardian*, "This is not a deeply analytical book. The points it makes are pretty obvious points. It is not a huge intellectual exercise. It's really just a book about what an interesting state childhood is and what an interesting and promising place the United States was 50 years ago and how I think it's kind of gone wrong."

Nowhere does that sentiment come across more clearly than in the final chapter, "Farewell." Here, nostalgia and history are again intertwined, as Bryson tolls the bell for all of those Des Moines and Iowa and midwestern and American institutions that formed his world yet no longer exist: the downtown movie palaces; Riverview Park, a local amusement park; Bishop's Buffet and other local restaurants; the *Tribune*, the evening paper for which his parents worked and which he "lugged thanklessly from house to house for so many years"; neighborhood stores; the great downtown department and clothing stores, including, finally, Younkers, which "in the end had only sixty employees."

Bryson hoped to find photographs of all of these places in the archives of the *Register* and the *Tribune*, but he discovered to his dismay that they had all been "recycled for the silver in the paper," as the paper's librarian tells him. "So now," he noted sadly, "not only are the places mostly gone, but there is no record of them either"—except, of course, for *The Life and Times of the Thunderbolt Kid*.

Kirkus Review declared that *Thunderbolt Kid* "combines nostalgia, sharp wit and a dash of hyperbole" and compared Bryson's "homespun, idiosyncratic voice" to that of Jean Shepherd, the midwestern author and radio star best remembered today for writing the short stories that became the basis for the 1983 movie *A Christmas Story*. *Biography* noted that Bryson's "primary purpose, even in recounting the story of himself, is to give the reader a good time," resulting in "an entertaining romp of a book." The *New York Times Book Review* humorously noted that the book is "so outlandishly and improbably entertaining, you begin to doubt its veracity." The exaggerations that Bryson employs in the text reveal "a much larger truth, a shocking revelation that few memoirists have been so brave to admit: he had a happy childhood." The *Spectator* review argues, however, that "the charm of the book resides solely in Bryson's gentle, humorous descriptions of his real and imaginary childhood adventures" and expresses annoyance at "the bits explaining how 1950s America was the best country in the world." Similarly, *Publishers Weekly*, in a review that is positive overall, claims that, because of Bryson's comic hyperbole, the book "can only be considered [a memoir] in the broadest sense." The historical material amounts to a "glib pop history of the decade, which works fine when discussing teen culture or the Cold War but falls flat when trying to rope in the Civil Rights movement."

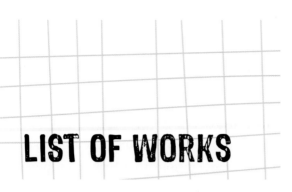

LIST OF WORKS

The Book of Blunders. New York: Dell, 1982.

The Facts on File Dictionary of Troublesome Words. New York: Facts on File, 1984; rev. ed. 1987. Published in England as *The Penguin Dictionary of Troublesome Words.*

The Palace under the Alps: And Over Two Hundred Other Unusual, Unspoiled, and Infrequently Visited Spots in Sixteen European Countries. New York: Congdon and Weed, 1985.

The Lost Continent: Travels in Small-Town America. New York: Harper and Row, 1989.

The Mother Tongue: English and How It Got That Way. New York: Morrow, 1990.

The Penguin Dictionary for Writers and Editors. New York: Viking, 1991; rev. ed. 1994. An expanded edition of *The Penguin Dictionary of Troublesome Words.*

Neither Here nor There: Travels in Europe. New York: Morrow, 1992.

Made in America: An Informal History of the English Language in the United States. New York: Morrow, 1994.

Notes from a Small Island: An Affectionate Portrait of Britain. New York: Morrow, 1995.

A Walk in the Woods: Rediscovering America on the Appalachian Trail. New York: Broadway Books, 1998.

I'm a Stranger Here Myself: Notes on Returning to America after Twenty Years Away. New York: Broadway Books, 1999. Published in England as *Notes from a Big Country.*

In a Sunburned Country. New York: Broadway Books, 2000. Published in England as *Down Under.*

Bryson's Dictionary of Troublesome Words. New York: Broadway Books, 2002. A revision of *The Facts on File Dictionary of Troublesome Words.*

Bill Bryson's African Diary. New York: Broadway Books, 2002.

A Short History of Nearly Everything. New York: Broadway Books, 2003; illustrated ed., 2005.

The Life and Times of the Thunderbolt Kid: A Memoir. New York: Broadway Books, 2006.

Shakespeare: The World as Stage. New York: HarperCollins, 2007; illustrated and updated ed., 2009.

Bryson's Dictionary for Writers and Editors. New York: Broadway Books, 2008. Revision of *The Penguin Dictionary for Writers and Editors.*

A Really Short History of Nearly Everything. Scarborough, ON: Doubleday Canada, 2008.

At Home: A Short History of Domestic Life. New York: Doubleday, 2010.

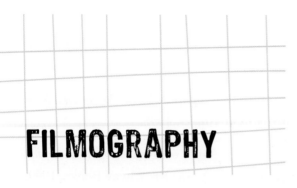

FILMOGRAPHY

Notes from a Small Island. Carlton Television. First broadcast January 10, 1999.

"Notes on a Dirty Island." *Panorama.* BBC One. First broadcast August 11, 2008.

CHRONOLOGY

1951 William McGuire Bryson is born in Des Moines, Iowa (December 8).

1969 Graduates from high school and enrolls at Drake University in Des Moines.

1972 Spends summer backpacking through Europe.

1973 Returns to Europe and first arrives in England on March 21. Spends April through August backpacking through Europe with "Stephen Katz." Settles in England in August and begins work at Holloway Sanatorium.

1975 Marries Cynthia Billen. Returns to the United States with his wife to complete his degree.

1977 Receives a B.A. in political science from Drake University. Returns to England with his wife and settles in Bournemouth. Is hired as a subeditor at the *Bournemouth Evening Echo*.

1979 The Brysons move to London, where Bryson is hired by the *Financial Times*.

1981 Is hired as a subeditor of the London *Times*; later becomes chief subeditor of the business section.

1982 *The Book of Blunders* is published (as Bill Bryson Jr.).

1984 *The Penguin Dictionary of Troublesome Words* is published.

1985 *The Palace under the Alps: And Over Two Hundred Other Unusual, Unspoiled, and Infrequently Visited Spots in Sixteen European Countries* is published (as William Bryson).

1986 Bryson's father dies. Bryson becomes deputy national news editor of the business section of the *Independent*; later becomes assistant home editor.

1987 Bryson takes the eastern leg of the cross-country trip that becomes the basis for *The Lost Continent*. Quits the *Independent* to become a full-time writer. The Brysons move to the Yorkshire Dales.

1988 Takes the western leg of the cross-country trip that becomes the basis for *The Lost Continent*.

1989 *The Lost Continent* is published.

1990 *The Mother Tongue* is published.

1991 *The Penguin Dictionary for Writers and Editors* is published.

1992 *Neither Here nor There* is published.

1994 *Made in America* is published. Bryson takes a seven-week trip around Britain (the basis for *Notes from a Small Island*).

1995 The Brysons move to Hanover, New Hampshire. *Notes from a Small Island* is published.

1996 Bryson hikes 870 miles of the Appalachian Trail, much of it with "Stephen Katz"; the trip later forms the basis of *A Walk in the Woods*. Bryson begins writing a weekly column for London's *Mail on Sunday* (September 1996–September 1998).

1998 *A Walk in the Woods* is published.

1999 *Notes from a Small Island*, a Carlton Television adaptation of Bryson's book of the same name, first airs on British television in January. *I'm a Stranger Here Myself*, a collection of Bryson's columns for the *Mail on Sunday*, is published.

2000 *In a Sunburned Country* is published. Bryson writes a column for the London *Times* during the Summer Olympics (Sydney, Australia).

2002 Visits Kenya with CARE International. *Bill Bryson's African Diary* is published.

2003 *Notes from a Small Island* receives the World Book Day award in England. *A Short History of Nearly Everything* is published. The Brysons return to England and settle near Wymondham, Norfolk. Bryson is appointed a commissioner for English Heritage.

2004 Wins the Aventis Prize for science writing for *A Short History of Nearly Everything*. Receives an honorary degree, Doctor of Civil Law, from Durham University.

2005 Wins the Descartes Prize for Science Communication for *A Short History of Nearly Everything*. Begins the process of obtaining British citizenship. Is appointed chancellor of Durham University (April).

2006 Helps establish the Bill Bryson Prize of the Royal Society of Chemistry. *The Life and Times of the Thunderbolt Kid* is published. The mayor of Des Moines names October 21 Bill Bryson—"The Thunderbolt Kid"—Day. Bryson receives an OBE for his contributions to literature (December 13). Is named a Schwartz Visiting Fellow of the Pomfret School, in Connecticut, for the 2006–2007 academic year.

2007 Receives the James Joyce Award of the Literary and Historical Society of University College Dublin. *Shakespeare: The World as Stage* is published. Bryson is appointed president of the Campaign to Protect Rural England.

2008 Films "Notes on a Dirty Island," an episode of the British television series *Panorama*. *A Really Short History of Nearly Everything* is published.

NOTES

Throughout the manuscript, all references to Bill Bryson's works refer to the following editions:

The Lost Continent: Travels in Small-Town America, New York: Harper and Row, 1989.

The Mother Tongue: English and How It Got That Way, New York: Morrow, 1990.

Neither Here nor There: Travels in Europe, New York: Morrow, 1992.

Made in America: An Informal History of the English Language in the United States, New York: Morrow, 1994.

Notes from a Small Island: An Affectionate Portrait of Britain, New York: Morrow, 1995.

A Walk in the Woods: Rediscovering America on the Appalachian Trail, New York: Broadway Books, 1998.

I'm a Stranger Here Myself: Notes on Returning to America after Twenty Years Away, New York: Broadway Books, 1999.

In a Sunburned Country, New York: Broadway Books, 2000.

Bryson's Dictionary of Troublesome Words, New York: Broadway Books, 2002.

A Short History of Nearly Everything, New York: Broadway Books, 2003.

The Life and Times of the Thunderbolt Kid: A Memoir, New York: Broadway Books, 2006.

Shakespeare: The World as Stage, New York: Atlas Books, 2007.

Chapter 1: Life

p. 7, James Thurber, Robert...": "He Loves Us, Too," *Telegraph* (UK), September 3, 2003.

p. 9, "During high school . . . ": Daisy Price, "How I Got Here: Bill Bryson," *Independent*, February 15, 2001.

p. 11, "Much as I . . . ": Norman Oder, "Bill Bryson: An Expat Traveling Light," *Publishers Weekly,* May 4, 1998.

p. 14, "summit of High Victorian. . . ": Ian Nairn and Nikolaus Pevsner, *Surrey*, New Haven: Yale University Press, 1971, 314.

p. 16, "it never really occurred to. . . ": Price, "How I Got Here," February 15, 2001.

p. 17, "considerably more left wing . . . ": Sathnam Sanghera, "Bill Bryson," *Financial Times*, December 6, 2003.

p. 17, "out of deference to his father. . . ": "He Loves Us, Too," *Telegraph* (UK), September 3, 2003.

p. 17, "Gradually I began . . . ": Price, "How I Got Here," February 15, 2001.

p. 17, "vainly seeking a veneer . . . ": Oder, "Bill Bryson: An Ex-expat Traveling Light," May 4, 1998.

p. 18, "instantly remaindered . . . ": Oder, "Bill Bryson: An Ex-expat Traveling Light," May 4, 1998.

p. 18, "I quit my job as . . . ": Price, "How I Got Here," February 15, 2001.

p. 18, "a very big gamble . . . ": Price, "How I Got Here," February 15, 2001.

p. 20, "its savage take on . . . ": Oder, "Bill Bryson: An Ex-expat Traveling Light," May 4, 1998.

p. 20, "some reviewers chided Bryson . . . ": Oder, "Bill Bryson: An Ex-expat Traveling Light," May 4, 1998.

p. 23, "*Notes from a Small Island* was an immediate. . . ": Maev Kennedy, "'From the Day He Came to Us It Was Obvious He Has a Deep Knowledge and an Absolute Passion for England's Heritage,'" *Guardian*, May 4, 2007.

p. 23, "pining for Radio 4 . . . ": Kennedy, *Guardian*, May 4, 2007.

p. 27, "By May 2007 this engagingly. . . ": Kennedy, *Guardian*, May 4, 2007.

p. 28, "He's just been to Kenya . . . ": Simon Hattenstone, "'You Have Only So Many Jokes,'" *Guardian*, November 22, 2002.

p. 28, "become a brand . . . ": John Gibbens, "How Man of Letters Became the Man of Litter," *Telegraph* (London), April 20, 2008.

p. 28, "With every passing month . . . ": Oder, "Bill Bryson: An Ex-expat Traveling Light," May 4, 1998.

p. 29, "no urge . . . ": Sanghera, "Bill Bryson," December 6, 2003.

p. 29, "they'll probably turn me down . . . ": John Crace, "Bill Bryson: The Accidental Chancellor," *Guardian*, November 15, 2005.

p. 29, "Every morning of my life . . . ": Kennedy, *Guardian*, May 4, 2007.

p. 30, "I can't quite believe . . . ": Crace, "Bill Bryson: The Accidental Chancellor," November 15, 2005.

p. 31, "Despite having been born . . . ": BBC.co.uk, "Bill Bryson Made an Honorary OBE," *BBC News,* December 13, 2006. http://news.bbc.co.uk/2/hi/entertainment/6176363. stm (accessed August 21, 2009).

p. 32, "We've already had . . . ": Kennedy, *Guardian*, May 4, 2007.

p. 34, "We are not asking you . . . ": *Marketing* (UK), "Profile: Clean-up crusader—Bill Bryson, President, Campaign to Protect Rural England, and Author," April 23, 2008, 24.

p. 34, "There is a lot . . . ": Sam Williams, "Bill Bryson Hits Out at Eco-Town Plan," November 7, 2008, www. eveningnews24.co.uk (accessed August 21, 2009).

p. 35, "I have a finite amount . . . ": Chuck Leddy, "Around the World (and Universe) with Bill Bryson," *The Writer*, January 2007, 16.

p. 35, "would very much prefer it if . . . ": Sanghera, "Bill Bryson," December 6, 2003.

p. 35, "I want to be home . . . ": Leddy, "Around the World (and Universe) with Bill Bryson," January 2007, 16.

p. 35, "a writer's life is . . . ": Leddy, "Around the World (and Universe) with Bill Bryson," January 2007, 16.

Chapter 2: Times

p. 37, "'Tyrannies,' Luce wrote, 'may require . . . '": Henry Luce, "The American Century," *Life*, February 17, 1941.

p. 38, "cannot come out of . . . ": Luce, "The American Century," February 17, 1941.

p. 38, "It must be an internationalism . . .": Luce, "The American Century," February 17, 1941.

p. 43, "from 26 percent in 1950 . . . ": George Gilder, "Women in the Work Force," *Atlantic*, September 1986.

p. 43, "at the end of . . . ": Gilder, "Women in the Work Force," September 1986.

p. 43, "by 1985 the census . . . ": Gilder, "Women in the Work Force," September 1986.

p. 43, "women comprised 46% . . . ": U.S. Department of Labor, Bureau of Labor Statistics, "Employment and Earnings: 2007 Annual Averages," www.bls.gov (accessed August 21, 2009).

p. 45, "While spending was . . . ": U.S. Department of Labor, Bureau of Labor Statistics, "One Hundred Years of U.S. Consumer Spending: Data for the Nation, New York City, and Boston," May 2006, www.bls.gov/opub/uscs/home.htm (accessed August 21, 2009).

p. 45, "Average family size declined ... ": U.S. Department of Labor, "One Hundred Years of U.S. Consumer Spending," May 2006.

p. 46, "The median age . . . ": U.S. Department of Labor, "One Hundred Years of U.S. Consumer Spending," May 2006.

p. 46, "59 percent of households . . . ": U.S. Department of Labor, "One Hundred Years of U.S. Consumer Spending," May 2006.

p. 54, "Adjusted for inflation . . . ": U.S. Department of Labor, "One Hundred Years of U.S. Consumer Spending," May 2006.

p. 57, "Clinton's performance as . . . ": Simon Hattenstone, "'You Have Only So Many Jokes,'" *Guardian*, November 22, 2002.

p. 58, "I am not a terribly moralistic . . . ": Hattenstone, "'You Have Only So Many Jokes,'" November 22, 2002.

p. 58, "may be a more decent ... ": Hattenstone, "'You Have Only So Many Jokes,'" November 22, 2002.

p. 58, "'Not so,' he told the Guardian, 'though obviously ... ": John Crace, "Bill Bryson: The Accidental Chancellor," *Guardian*, November 15, 2005.

p. 59, "I'm a little worried that . . . ": Crace, "Bill Bryson: The Accidental Chancellor," November 15, 2005.

Chapter 3: Works

p. 61, "I stumbled into this genre . . . ": Norman Oder, "Bill Bryson: An Ex-expat Traveling Light," *Publishers Weekly,* May 4, 1998.

p. 61, "acknowledges that *The Lost* . . . ": Oder, "Bill Bryson: An Ex-expat Traveling Light," May 4, 1998.

pp. 68–69, "Bryson's book is a marvelous . . . ": Ron Antonucci, "A Walk in the Woods: Rediscovering America on the Appalachian Trail," *Booklist*, April 1998, 1297.

p. 69, "Bryson shares some truly . . . ": Nancy J. Moeckel, "A Walk in the Woods: Rediscovering America on the Appalachian Trail," *Library Journal*, April 1, 1998, 114.

p. 69, "is a blend of personal . . . ": Nancy Pearl, "Something To Talk About: Book Group Reads," *Library Journal*, September 15, 2001, 140.

p. 69, "records the misadventure . . . ": "A Walk in the Woods: Rediscovering America on the Appalachian Trail,'" *Publishers Weekly*, February 23, 1998, 57.

p. 69, "casually and comfortably . . . ": *New Statesman*, December 12, 1997, 43.

p. 79, "a language maven . . . ": Chuck Leddy, "Bryson Offers a Pithy, Common-Sense Guide to Usage," *The Writer*, July 2003, 46.

p. 79, "blend of linguistic anecdote . . . ": Genevieve Stuttaford, "The Mother Tongue: English and How It Got That Way," *Publishers Weekly*, May 25, 1990, 46.

p. 79, "English can survive anything . . . ": Christopher Lehmann-Haupt, "English: A Linguistic Success Story," *New York Times*, July 16, 1990.

p. 90, "a mind-bending odyssey . . . ": Don McLeese, "Universe in a Nutshell," *Book*, July–August 2003, 76.

p. 90, "there are people much better . . . ": Robert Macfarlane, "Gluons, Bosons and Quarks," *Spectator*, June 7, 2003, 37.

p. 90, "a man who knows . . . ": "A Short History of Nearly Everything (Nonfiction)," *Kirkus Reviews*, April 1, 2003, 517.

p. 91, "great for Bryson . . . ": "A Short History of Nearly Everything, (Nonfiction)," *Publishers Weekly*, April 7, 2003, 59.

p. 91, "Although Bryson clearly intends . . . ": James Olson, "Bryson, Bill. A Short History of Nearly Everything," *Library Journal*, May 15, 2003, 120.

p. 93, "There was a real . . . ": Emma Brockes, "Travels with a Super Hero," *Guardian*, September 2, 2006.

pp. 99–100, "This is not a deeply . . . ": Brockes, "Travels with a Super Hero," September 2, 2006.

p. 100, "combines nostalgia, sharp wit and . . . ": "Bryson, Bill: The Life and Times of the Thunderbolt Kid: A Memoir," *Kirkus Reviews*, July 1, 2006, 660.

p. 101, "primary purpose, even in . . . ": Bruce McCall, "The Life and Times of the Thunderbolt Kid," *Biography*, Winter 2007, 124.

p. 101, "so outlandishly and improbably . . . ": Jay Jennings, "Happy Days," *New York Times Book Review*, October 15, 2006, 9.

p. 101, "the charm of the book . . . ": Zenga Longmore, "Happy days in Middle America," *Spectator*, September 30, 2006.

p. 101, "can only be considered . . . ": "The Life and Times of the Thunderbolt Kid: A Memoir," *Publishers Weekly*, July 10, 2006, 61.

FURTHER INFORMATION

Websites

Archive of articles by and about Bill Bryson at the *Guardian*
www.guardian.co.uk/books/billbryson

Bill Bryson's Home Page at Durham University
www.dur.ac.uk/bill.bryson/

Metacritic.com Reviews of *The Life and Times of the Thunderbolt Kid*
www.metacritic.com/books/authors/brysonbill/lifeand timesofthethunderboltkid

Official UK Website for Bill Bryson
www.booksattransworld.co.uk/billbryson/

Official U.S. Website for Bill Bryson
www.randomhouse.com/features/billbryson/

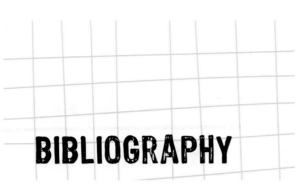

BIBLIOGRAPHY

Antonucci, Ron. Review of *A Walk in the Woods: Rediscovering America on the Appalachian Trail*, by Bill Bryson. *Booklist*, April 1998, 1297.

BBC.co.uk. "Bill Bryson Made an Honorary OBE." BBC News, December 13, 2006. http://news.bbc.co.uk/2/hi/entertainment/6176363.stm (accessed August 21, 2009).

Brockes, Emma. "Travels with a Super Hero." *Guardian* (UK), September 2, 2006.

Crace, John. "Bill Bryson: The Accidental Chancellor." *Guardian* (UK), November 15, 2005.

Gibbens, John. "How Man of Letters Became the Man of Litter." *Telegraph* (London), April 20, 2008.

Gilder, George. "Women in the Work Force." *Atlantic,* September 1986.

Hattenstone, Simon. "'You Have Only So Many Jokes.'" *Guardian* (UK), November 22, 2002.

Jennings, Jay. "Happy Days." Review of *The Life and Times*

of the Thunderbolt Kid: A Memoir, by Bill Bryson. *New York Times Book Review,* October 15, 2006, 9.

Kennedy, Maev. "'From the Day He Came to Us It Was Obvious He Has a Deep Knowledge and an Absolute Passion for England's Heritage.'" *Guardian* (UK), May 4, 2007.

Kirkus Reviews. Review of *The Life and Times of the Thunderbolt Kid: A Memoir*, by Bill Bryson. July 1, 2006, 660.

Kirkus Reviews. Review of *A Short History of Nearly Everything*, by Bill Bryson. April 1, 2003, 517.

Leddy, Chuck. "Around the World (and Universe) with Bill Bryson." *Writer,* January 2007, 16.

Lehmann-Haupt, Christopher. "English: A Linguistic Success Story." Review of *The Mother Tongue: English and How It Got That Way*, by Bill Bryson. *New York Times,* July 16, 1990.

Longmore, Zenga. "Happy Days in Middle America." Review of *The Life and Times of the Thunderbolt Kid: A Memoir*, by Bill Bryson. *Spectator* (UK), September 30, 2006.

Luce, Henry. "The American Century." *Life,* February 17, 1941.

Macfarlane, Robert. "Gluons, Bosons and Quarks." Review of *A Short History of Nearly Everything*, by Bill Bryson. Spectator (UK), June 7, 2003, 37.

Marketing (UK). "Profile: Clean-up Crusader—Bill Bryson, President, Campaign to Protect Rural England, and Author." April 23, 2008, 24.

McCall, Bruce. Review of *The Life and Times of the Thunderbolt Kid: A Memoir*, by Bill Bryson. *Biography*, Winter 2007, 124.

McLeese, Don. "Universe in a Nutshell." Review of *A Short History of Nearly Everything*, by Bill Bryson. *Book*, July–August 2003, 76.

Moeckel, Nancy J. Review of *A Walk in the Woods: Rediscovering America on the Appalachian Trail*, by Bill Bryson. *Library Journal*, April 1, 1998, 114.

Nairn, Ian, and Nikolaus Pevsner. *Surrey.* New Haven, CT: Yale University Press, 1971.

Oder, Norman. "Bill Bryson: An Ex-Expat Traveling Light." *Publishers Weekly,* May 4, 1998.

Olson, James. Review of *A Short History of Nearly Everything*, by Bill Bryson. *Library Journal,* May 15, 2003, 120.

Pearl, Nancy. "Something to Talk About: Book Group Reads." Review of *A Walk in the Woods: Rediscovering America on the Appalachian Trail*, by Bill Bryson. *Library Journal,* September 15, 2001, 140.

Price, Daisy. "How I Got Here: Bill Bryson." *Independent* (UK), February 15, 2001.

Publishers Weekly. Review of *The Life and Times of the Thunderbolt Kid: A Memoir*, by Bill Bryson. July 10, 2006, 61.

Publishers Weekly. Review of *A Short History of Nearly Everything*, by Bill Bryson. April 7, 2003, 59.

Publishers Weekly. Review of *A Walk in the Woods: Rediscovering America on the Appalachian Trail*, by Bill Bryson. February 23, 1998, 57.

Sanghera, Sathnam. "Bill Bryson." *Financial Times* (London), December 6, 2003.

Scardino, Albert. Review of *A Walk in the Woods: Rediscovering America on the Appalachian Trail. New Statesman* (UK). December 12, 1997, 43.

Stuttaford, Genevieve. Review of *The Mother Tongue: English and How It Got That Way*, by Bill Bryson. *Publishers Weekly*, May 25, 1990, 46.

Telegraph (London). "He Loves Us, Too." September 3, 2003.

U.S. Department of Labor, Bureau of Labor Statistics. "Employment and Earnings: 2007 Annual Averages." www.bls.gov (accessed August 21, 2009).

———. "One Hundred Years of U.S. Consumer Spending: Data for the Nation, New York City, and Boston." May 2006, www.bls.gov/opub/uscs/home.htm (accessed August 21, 2009).

Williams, Sam. "Bill Bryson Hits Out at Eco-Town Plan." November 7, 2008, www.eveningnews24.co.uk (accessed August 21, 2009).

INDEX

ABOUT THE AUTHOR

SCOTT P. RICHERT is the executive editor of *Chronicles: A Magazine of American Culture* and the Catholicism Guide for About.com. His monthly column in *Chronicles*, "The Rockford Files," examines political, economic, social, and cultural trends in America from the vantage point of a middle-sized town in the midwest. A graduate of Michigan State University, he holds an M.A. in political theory from the Catholic University of America. He lives in Rockford, Illinois, with his wife, Amy, and their seven children. He has previously contributed to two of our Marshall Cavendish Reference sets. *Bill Bryson* is his first book for Marshall Cavendish Benchmark.

DATE DUE